To Quote
C.S. Lewis

To Quote
C.S. Lewis

COMPILED BY
OWEN COLLINS

Fount
An Imprint of HarperCollins*Publishers*

Fount is an Imprint of
HarperCollins*Religious*
part of HarperCollins*Publishers*
77–85 Fulham Palace Road, London W6 8JB
www.christian-publishing.com

First published in Great Britain in 2000
by HarperCollins*Publishers*

1 3 5 7 9 10 8 6 4 2

A catalogue record for this book is
available from the British Library

ISBN 0 00 628168 0

Contents

Introduction

For the countless fans of C.S. Lewis (1898–1963) who exist today, nearly forty years after his death, this Oxford professor and author needs no introduction. They will readily recall that C.S. Lewis died a week before his sixty-fifth birthday, on the afternoon of Friday 22 November 1963, the same day as the assassination of President Kennedy.

C.S. Lewis's admirers claim that he is perhaps the most widely read Christian intellectual of the twentieth century. For the past forty years over two million of his books have sold each year on both sides of the Atlantic. Some would go so far as to argue that C.S. Lewis was the most influential Christian author of the twentieth century.

This collection brings together over two hundred of quotations from more than forty of Lewis's various books, together with extracts from some of his letters and his spoken words. Fifty of his well-known one-liners are also included. Many of these are found in the following quotations, which thus give the context to the one-liners. *The Screwtape Letters* are a series of letters from Screwtape, an experienced devil, giving advice to Wormwood, a junior devil. So the quotations from this book need to be read from the senior devil's viewpoint, in that 'the Enemy', according to Screwtape, is God.

Dr J.I. Packer asked the following question about C.S. Lewis: 'Why was Lewis so uncannily prophetic?' He answered his own question in this way:

> *The answer may be somewhat discomfiting to modern evangelicals: One reason is precisely that Lewis was* not *an evangelical. He was a professor in the academy, with a specialty in medieval literature, which gave him a mental framework shaped by the whole scope of intellectual history and Christian thought. As a result, he was liberated from the narrow confines of the world-view of his own age – which meant he was able to analyse and critique it.*

Packer went on to state that:

> *His strength lay not in the forming of new ideas but in the arresting simplicity, both logical and imaginative, with which he projected old ones. Not wasting words, he plunged straight into things and boiled matters down to essentials, positioning himself as a common-sense, down-to-earth, no-nonsense observer, analyst,*

and conversation partner ... At his best, Lewis is a teacher of great piercing power.

Packer then asks another question: 'What is his secret?' His answer:

The secret lies in the blend of logic and imagination in Lewis's make-up, each power as strong as the other, and each enormously strong in its own right. The best teachers are always those in whom imagination and logical control combine, so that you receive wisdom from their flights of fancy as well as a human heartbeat from their logical analyses and arguments. This in fact is human communication at its profoundest, for in the sending-receiving process both lobes of the brain (left for logic, right for imagination) are engaged.[1]

Clive Staples Lewis ('Jack' Lewis to his friends) was, in the estimation of many, the most popular and most effective explainer and defender of the Christian faith writing in English in the twentieth century. He tried to make a point of avoiding disputes on matters where Christians disagree and defending those beliefs which they hold in common. His work was valued by many Christians of widely differing backgrounds: Anglican, Baptist, Methodist, Pentecostal, Presbyterian, Roman Catholic and others.

---

[1] *Christianity Today,* 7 September 1998, vol. 42, no. 10, p. 54. From an article entitled 'Still surprised by Lewis: why the non-evangelical Oxford don has become our patron saint' by Dr J. I. Packer.

This collection of quotations from the pen of the professor who once described himself as 'tall, fat, bald, red-faced, double-chinned, black-haired and wear glasses for reading' is intended for lovers of C.S. Lewis, for lovers of collections of quotations, and for lovers of succinct, positive quotations about Christianity and life.

Owen Collins

A brief chronology

1898   Born 29 November in Belfast, Ireland.

1905   The Lewis family move to 'Little Lea' on the outskirts
        of Belfast.

1908   Lewis's mother, Florence Lewis, dies of cancer on 23
        August. In September he is sent to school at Wynyard
        in Watford, Hertfordshire, England.

1910   Lewis goes to Campbell College in Ireland.

1911   Returns to England and attends school at Cherbourg
        House, Malvern.

1913   Enters Malvern College

1914   Tutored by W.T. Kirkpatrick for Oxford. Meets Joseph
        Arthur Greeves, who becomes a lifelong friend. They
        write to each other for forty-nine years.

1915   Reads George MacDonald's *Phantastes* which 'baptizes'
        his imagination.

1916   Wins a scholarship to Oxford and gains a place at
        University College. To his father he writes, 'This place
        has surpassed my wildest dreams; I never saw anything
        so beautiful.'

1917   Begins his studies at University College, Oxford, in
        April, but is recruited into the army before the end of
        his first term. Commissioned a second lieutenant in the
        Somerset Light Infantry in September, he goes to the
        front in November.

1918   Suffers from trench fever, recovers only to be wounded
        in action at Mount Bernenchon, near Lilliers, in April
        and is hospitalized out of the war.

1919   Returns to University College and publishes *Spirits in
        Bondage* under the pseudonym of Clive Hamilton.

1920   Gains a First in Honour Moderations.

1922   Gains a First in Greats (classics and philosophy), and is
        awarded his BA degree.

1923   Gains a First in English Language and Literature,
        winning the Chancellor's Prize for an English essay.

1924   Becomes a tutor at University College.

1925   Elected Fellow in English Language and Literature at
        Magdalen College, Oxford. He remains there for the
        next thirty years.

1926   Publishes the narrative poem *Dymer* under the
        pseudonym Clive Hamilton.

1929   His father, Albert J. Lewis, dies in Belfast. Lewis
        becomes a theist.

1931   Lewis believes that Jesus Christ is the Son of God. He becomes a regular communicant member of the Church of England.

1933   Publishes *The Pilgrim's Regress: An Allegorical Apology for Christianity, Reason and Romanticism* under his own name, dropping the Clive Hamilton pseudonym for ever.

1936   Publishes *The Allegory of Love: A Study in Medieval Tradition,* which wins him the Hawthornden Prize.

1938   Publishes *Out of the Silent Planet.*

1939   Publishes *The Personal Heresy: A Controversy,* with E.M.W. Tillyard; publishes *Rehabilitations and Other Essays.*

1940   Publishes *The Problem of Pain.* Wartime lecturer to the Royal Air Force. Lectures to them on Christianity.

1941   Begins a series of twenty-one talks on BBC radio.

1942   Publishes *Broadcast Talks* from his radio lectures. Publishes *The Screwtape Letters* and *A Preface to 'Paradise Lost'.*

1943   Publishes *Perelandra* and *The Abolition of Man,* and additional BBC radio lectures under the title of *Christian Behaviour.*

1944   Publishes *Beyond Personality,* later incorporated into *Mere Christianity.*

1945   Publishes *The Great Divorce* and *That Hideous Strength.*

1946   Edits *George MacDonald: An Anthology.*

1947   Is awarded a Doctorate of Divinity by St Andrews

University, Scotland, for his anthology of George MacDonald. Publishes *Miracles: A Preliminary Study*.

1948   Publishes *Arthurian Torso*.

1949   Publishes *Transposition and Other Addresses*. This collection of some of Lewis's finest essays is published in America under the title *The Weight of Glory and Other Addresses*.

1950   Receives his first letter from Joy Davidman. Publishes *The Lion, the Witch and the Wardrobe*, which becomes the first of seven Narnia stories.

1951   Publishes *Prince Caspian: The Return to Narnia*.

1952   Meets Joy Davidman. Publishes *Mere Christianity*, which includes *Broadcast Talks*, *Christian Behaviour* and *Beyond Personality*. Publishes *The Voyage of the 'Dawn Treader'*.

1953   Publishes *The Silver Chair*.

1954   Publishes *The Horse and His Boy* and *English Literature in the Sixteenth Century Excluding Drama*.

1955   Is appointed Professor of Medieval and Renaissance Literature at Magdalene College, Cambridge. Publishes *Surprised by Joy: The Shape of My Early Life* and *The Magician's Nephew*.

1956   Marries Joy Davidman Gresham in a civil ceremony in April. Publishes *The Last Battle* and *Till We Have Faces: A Myth Retold*, which Lewis regarded as his best book.

1957   Marries Joy Davidman in an Anglican ceremony in March at her hospital bedside where she is suffering from cancer. The hospital send Joy home 'to die', but Lewis believes that she has been miraculously healed through prayer and the laying on of hands at her bedside.

1958   Publishes *Reflections on the Psalms*.

1960   Publishes *The Four Loves, Studies in Words*, and *The World's Last Night and Other Essays*. Joy dies on 13 July.

1961   Publishes *A Grief Observed* under the pen name of N.W. Clerk. Publishes *An Experiment in Criticism*.

1962   Publishes *They Asked for a Paper: Papers and Addresses*, a collection of twelve essays.

1963   Dies on 22 November, the same day Aldous Huxley and John F. Kennedy died.

1964   *Letters to Malcolm: Chiefly on Prayer*, finished in 1963, is published.

Full details of the writings of C.S. Lewis can be found in *C.S. Lewis: A Companion and Guide*, by Walter Hooper, published by HarperCollins in 1996. Page references in this book are taken from Fount's centenary editions, published from 1998 onwards.

Quotations by subject

ABIDING IN CHRIST

... a Christian can lose the Christ-life which has been put into him, and he has to make efforts to keep it. But even the best Christian that ever lived is not acting on his own steam – he is only nourishing or protecting a life he could never have acquired by his own efforts. And that has practical consequences. As long as the natural life is in your body, it will do a lot towards repairing that body. Cut it, and up to a point it will heal, as a dead body would not. A live body is not one that never gets hurt, but one that can to some extent repair itself. In the same way a Christian is not a man who never goes wrong, but a man who is enabled to repent and pick himself up and begin over again after each stumble – because the Christ-life is inside him, repairing him all the time, enabling him to repeat (in some degree) the kind of voluntary death which Christ Himself carried out.

Mere Christianity, p. 52

AFFECTION

Affection ... is the humblest love. It gives itself no airs. People can be proud of being 'in love', or of friendship. Affection is modest – even furtive and shame-faced.

The Four Loves, p. 32

If we try to live by Affection alone, Affection will 'go bad on us' ... If Affection is made the absolute sovereign of a human life the seeds will germinate. Love, having become a god, becomes a demon.

The Four Loves, pp. 52–3

APOLOGETICS

We are to defend Christianity itself – the faith preached by the Apostles, attested by the Martyrs, embodied in the

Creeds, expounded by the Fathers. This must be clearly distinguished from the whole of what any one of us may think about God and Man. Each of us has his individual emphasis: each holds, in addition to the Faith, many opinions which seem to him to be consistent with it and true and important. And so perhaps they are. But as apologists it is not our business to defend *them*. We are defending Christianity; not 'my religion'.

'Christian Apologetics' in *Compelling Reason*, p. 63

... you must translate every bit of your Theology into the vernacular. This is very troublesome and it means you can say very little in half an hour, but it is essential. It is also of the greatest service to your own thought. I have come to the conviction that if you cannot translate your thoughts into uneducated language, then your thoughts were confused. Power to translate is the test of having really understood one's own meaning. A passage from some theological work for translation into the vernacular ought to be a compulsory paper in every Ordination examination.

'Christian Apologetics' in *Compelling Reason*, p. 72

Do not attempt to water Christianity down. There must be no pretence that you can have it with the Supernatural left out. So far as I can see Christianity is precisely the one religion from which the miraculous cannot be separated. You must frankly argue for supernaturalism from the outset.

'Christian Apologetics' in *Compelling Reason*, p. 73

I have found that nothing is more dangerous to one's own faith than the work of an apologist. No doctrine of that Faith seems to me so spectral, so unreal as one that I have just successfully defended in a public debate. For a moment, you see, it has seemed to rest on oneself: as a result, when you go away from that debate, it seems no stronger than a weak pillar. That is why we apologists take our lives in our hands and can be saved only by falling back continually from the web of our own arguments, as from our intellectual counters, into the Reality – from Christian apologetics into Christ Himself. That also is why we need one another's continual help – *oremus pro invicem* [let us pray for each other].

'Christian Apologetics' in *Compelling Reason*, p. 77

Three letters by C.S. Lewis

The following letters by C.S. Lewis were written to Sheldon Vanauken, who wrote the best-selling book A Severe Mercy. *Mr Vanauken asked Lewis for the right to use the letters in his booklet* Encounter with Light, *and Lewis gave permission. Mr Vanauken subsequently put the letters in the public domain.*

Letter one: 14 December 1950

Dear Mr Vanauken,

My own position at the threshold of Xianity was exactly the opposite of yours. You wish it were true; I strongly hoped it was not. At least, that was my conscious wish: you may suspect that I had unconscious wishes of quite a different sort and that it was these which finally shoved me in. True: but then I may equally suspect that under your conscious wish that it were true, there lurks a strong unconscious wish that it were not. What this works out to is that all the modern thinking, however useful it may be for explaining the origin of an error which you already know to be an error, is perfectly useless in deciding which of two beliefs is the error and which is the truth. For (a) one never knows all one's wishes, and (b) in very big questions, such as this, even one's conscious wishes are nearly always engaged on both sides. What I think one can say with certainty is this: the notion that everyone would like Xianity to be true, and that therefore all atheists are brave men who have accepted the defeat of all their deepest desires, is simply impudent nonsense. Do you think people like Stalin, Hitler, Haldane, Stapledon (a corking good writer, by the way) wd. be pleased on waking up one morning to find that they were not their own masters, that they had a Master and a Judge, that there was nothing even in the deepest recesses of their thoughts about which they cd. say to Him 'Keep out! Private. This is my business'?

Do you? Rats! Their first reaction wd. be (as mine was) rage and terror. And I v. much doubt whether even you wd. find it simply pleasant. Isn't the truth this: that it wd. gratify some of our desires (ones we feel in fact pretty seldom) and outrage a good many others? So let's wash out all the wish business. It never helped anyone to solve any problem yet.

I don't agree with your picture of the history of religion. Christ, Buddha, Mohammed and others elaborating on an original simplicity. I believe Buddhism to be a simplification of Hinduism and Islam to be a simplification of Xianity. Clear, lucid, transparent, simple religion (Tao plus a shadowy, ethical god in the background) is a late development, usually arising among highly educated people in great cities. What you really start with is ritual, myth, and mystery, the death & return of Balder or Osiris, the dances, the initiations, the sacrifices, the divine kings. Over against that are the Philosophers, Aristotle or Confucius, hardly religion at all. The only two systems in which the mysteries and the philosophies come together are Hinduism and Xianity: there you get both the Metaphysics and Cult (continuous with primeval cults). That is why my first step was to be sure that one or the other of these had the answer. For the reality can't be one that appeals either only to savages or only to high brows. Real things aren't like that (e.g. matter is the first most obvious thing you meet; milk, chocolates, apples, and also the object of quantum physics). There is no question of just a crowd of disconnected religions. The choice is between

(a) The materialist world picture: wh. I can't believe. (b) The real archaic primitive religions; wh. are not moral enough. (c) The (claimed) fulfilment of these in Hinduism. (d) The claimed fulfilment of these in Xianity. But the weakness of Hinduism is that it doesn't really merge the two strands. Unredeemable savage religion goes on in the village; the Hermit philosophizes in the forest: and neither really interfaces with the other. It is only Xianity which compels a high brow like me to partake of a ritual blood feast, and also compels a central African convert to attempt an enlightened code of ethics.

Have you ever tried Chesterton's *The Everlasting Man?* The best popular apologetic I know.

Meanwhile, the attempt to practice Tao is certainly the right line. Have you read the Analects of Confucius? He ends up by saying, 'This is the Tao. I do not know if anyone has ever kept it.' That's significant: one can really go direct from there to the Epistle of the Romans.

I don't know if any of this is the least use. Be sure to write again, or call, if you think I can be of any help.

Yours sincerely

C.S. Lewis

Letter two: 23 December 1950

Dear Mr Vanauken,

The contradiction 'we must have faith to believe and must believe to have faith' belongs to the same class as those … philosophers [who] proved that all motion is impossible. And there are many others. You can't swim unless you can support yourself in water & you can't support yourself in water unless you can swim. Or again, in an act of volition (e.g. getting up in the morning) is the very beginning of the act itself voluntary or involuntary? If voluntary then you must have willed it, you were willing it already, it was not really the beginning. If involuntary, then the continuation of the act (being determined by the first movement) is involuntary too. But in spite of this we do swim, & we do get out of bed.

I do not think there is a demonstrative proof (like Euclid) of Christianity, nor of the existence of matter, nor of the good will & honesty of my best & oldest friends. I think all three (except perhaps the second) far more probable than the alternatives. The case for Xianity in general is well given by Chesterton; and I tried to do something in my Broadcast Talks. As to why God doesn't make it demonstrably clear; are we sure that He is even interested in the kind of Theism which wd. be a compelled logical assent to a conclusive argument? Are we interested in it in personal matters? I demand from my friend a trust in my good faith which is certain without demonstrative proof. It wouldn't be confidence at all if he waited for rigorous proof. Hang it all, the very fairy tales embody the truth. Othello believed in Desdemona's innocence when it was proved: but that was too late. 'His praise is lost who stays till all commend.' The magnanimity, the generosity which will trust on a reasonable probability, is required of us. But supposing one believed and was wrong after all? Why, then you wd. have paid the universe a compliment it doesn't deserve. Your error wd. even so be more interesting & important than the reality. And yet how cd. that be? How cd. an idiotic universe have produced creatures whose mere dreams are so much stronger, better, subtler than itself?

Note that life after death which still seems to you the essential thing, was itself a late revelation. God trained the Hebrews for centuries to believe in Him without promising them an afterlife, and, blessings on Him, he trained me in the same way for about a year. It is like the disguised prince in a fairy tale who wins the heroine's love before she knows he is anything more than a woodcutter. What wd. be a bribe if it came first had better come last.

It is quite clear from what you say that you have conscious wishes on both sides. And now, another point about wishes. A wish may lead to false beliefs, granted. But what does the existence of the wish suggest? At one time I was much impressed by Arnold's line 'Nor does the being hungry prove that we have bread.' But surely tho' it doesn't prove that one particular man will get food, it does prove that there is such a thing as food! i.e. if we were a species that didn't normally eat, weren't designed to eat, wd. we feel hungry? You say the materialist universe is 'ugly'. I wonder how you discovered that! If you are really a product of a materialistic universe, how is it you don't feel at home there? Do fish complain of the sea for being wet? Or if they did, would that fact itself not strongly suggest that they had not always, or wd. not always be, purely aquatic creatures? Notice how we are perpetually surprised at Time. ('How time flies! Fancy John being grown-up and married! I can hardly believe it!') In heaven's name, why? Unless, indeed, there is something about us that is not temporal.

Total humility is not in the Tao because the Tao (as such) says nothing about the Object to which it wd. be the right response: just as there is no law about railways in the acts of Q. Elizabeth. But from the degree of respect wh. the Tao demands for ancestors, parents, elders, & teachers, it is quite clear what the Tao wd. prescribe towards an object such as God.

But I think you are already in the meshes of the net! The Holy Spirit is after you. I doubt if you'll get away!

Yours,

C.S. Lewis

Letter three: 17 April 1951

Dear Vanauken,

My prayers are answered. No: a glimpse is not a vision. But to a man on a mountain road by night, a glimpse of the next three feet of road may matter more than a vision of the horizon. And there must perhaps be always just enough lack of demonstrative certainty to make free choice possible: for what could we do but accept if the faith were like the multiplication table?

There will be a counter attack on you, you know, so don't be too alarmed when it comes.

The enemy will not see you vanish into God's company without an effort to reclaim you.

Be busy learning to pray and (if you have made up yr. mind on the denominational question) get confirmed.

Blessings on you and a hundred thousand welcomes. Make use of me in any way you please: and let us pray for each other always.

Yours,

C.S. Lewis

ATHEISM

... atheism turns out to be too simple. If the whole universe has no meaning, we should have never found out that it has no meaning: Just as, if there were no light in the universe and therefore no creatures with eyes, we should never know it was dark. *Dark* would be without meaning.

Mere Christianity, p. 32

BEHAVIOUR, CHRISTIAN

An individual Christian may see fit to give up all sorts of things for special reasons – marriage, or meat, or beer, or the cinema; but the moment he starts saying the things are bad in themselves, or looking down his nose at other people who do use them, he has taken the wrong turning.

Mere Christianity, p. 65

Benevolence

The senior devil, Screwtape, wrote to his nephew Wormwood with advice on how to tempt and win a human being in Wormwood's charge. 'The Enemy' is God.

Do what you will, there is going to be some benevolence, as well as some malice, in your patient's soul. The great thing is to direct the malice to his immediate neighbours whom he meets every day and to thrust his benevolence out to the remote circumference, to people he does not know. The malice thus becomes wholly real and the benevolence largely imaginary ... Think of your man as a series of concentric circles, his will being the innermost, his intellect coming next, and finally his fantasy. You can hardly hope, at once, to exclude from all the circles everything that smells of the Enemy: but you must keep on shoving all the virtues outward till they are finally located in the circle of fantasy, and all the desirable qualities inward into the Will. It is only in so far as they reach the Will and are there embodied in habits that the virtues are really fatal to us.

The Screwtape Letters, p. 23

BLESSINGS

I am beginning to feel that we need a preliminary act of submission not only towards possible future afflictions but also towards possible future blessings. I know it sounds fantastic; but think it over. It seems to me that we often, almost sulkily, reject the good that God offers us because, at that moment, we expected some other good. Do you know what I mean? On every level of our life – in our religious experience, in our gastronomic, erotic, aesthetic and social experience – we are always harking back to some occasion which seemed to us to reach perfection, setting that up as a norm, and depreciating all other occasions by comparison. But these other occasions, I now suspect, are often full of their own new blessings if only we would lay ourselves open to it. God shows us a new facet of the glory, and we refuse to look at it because we're still looking for the old one. And of course we don't get that.

Letters to Malcolm: Chiefly on Prayer, p. 24

BODY, THE

Man has held three views of his body. First there is that of those ascetic Pagans who called it the prison or the 'tomb' of the soul, and of Christians like Fisher to whom it was a 'sack of dung', food for worms, filthy, shameful, a source of nothing but temptation to bad men and humiliation to good ones. Then there are the Neo-Pagans (they seldom know Greek), the nudist and the sufferers from Dark Gods, to whom the body is glorious. But thirdly we have the view which St Francis expressed by calling his body, 'Brother Ass'. All three may be – I am not sure – defensible; but give me St Francis for my money.

'Ass' is exquisitely right because no one in his senses can either revere or hate a donkey. It is a useful, sturdy, lazy, obstinate, patient, loveable and infuriating beast; deserving now the stick and now a carrot; both pathetically and absurdly beautiful. So the body. There's no living with it till we recognise that one of its functions in our lives is to play the part of buffoon. Until some theory has sophisticated them, every man, woman and child in the world knows this. The fact that we have bodies is the oldest joke there is ... The highest does not stand without the lowest. There is indeed at certain moments a high poetry in the flesh itself; but also, by your leave, an irreducible element of obstinate and ludicrous unpoetry. If it does not make itself felt on one occasion, it will on another. Far better to plant it foursquare within the drama of Eros as comic relief than pretend you haven't noticed it.

The Four Loves, pp. 96–7

15

CHASTITY

There is no getting away from it: the old Christian rule is 'Either marriage, with complete faithfulness to your partner, or else total abstinence.' Chastity is the most unpopular of our Christian virtues.

Mere Christianity, p. 79

CHRIST

The discrepancy between the depth and sanity and (let me add) *shrewdness* of His moral teaching and the rampant megalomania which must lie behind His theological teaching unless He is indeed God, has never been satisfactorily explained. Hence the non-Christian hypotheses succeed one another with the restless fertility of bewilderment. Today we are asked to regard all the theological elements as later accretions to the story of a 'historical' and merely human Jesus: yesterday we were asked to believe that the whole thing began with vegetation myths and mystery religions and that the pseudo-historical Man was only fadged up at a later date.

Miracles, p. 114

'What are we to make of Jesus Christ?' There is no question of what we can make of Him, it is entirely a question of what He intends to make of us. You must accept or reject the story.

The things He says are very different from what any other teacher has said. Others say, 'This is the truth about the Universe. This is the way you ought to go,' but He says, '*I* am the Truth, and the Way, and the Life.' He says, 'No man can reach absolute reality, except through Me. Try to retain your own life and you will be inevitably ruined. Give yourself away and you will be saved.' He says, 'If you are ashamed of Me, if, when you hear this call, you turn the other way, I also will look the other way when I come again as God without disguise. If anything whatever is keeping you from God and from Me, whatever it is, throw it away. If it is your eye, pull it out. If it is your hand, cut it off. If it is your self first you will be last. Come to Me everyone who is carrying a heavy load, I will set that right. Your sins, all of them, are wiped out, I can do that. I am Re-birth, I am Life. Eat Me, drink Me, I am your Food. And finally, do not be afraid, I have overcome the whole Universe.' That is the issue.

God in the Dock, p. 77

A man who was merely a man and said the sort of things Jesus said would not be a great moral teacher. He would be a lunatic – on a level with a man who says he is a poached egg – or else he would be the devil of Hell. You must make a choice. Either this man was, and is, the Son of God or else a madman or something worse. You can shut Him up for a fool, you can spit at Him and kill Him as a demon; or you can fall at his feet and call Him Lord and God. But let us not come up with any patronizing nonsense about His being a great human teacher. He has not left that open to us. He did not intend to.

Mere Christianity, p. 43

CHRIST, DEATH OF

We are told that Christ was killed for us, that His death has washed out our sins, and that by dying He disabled death itself. That is the formula. That is Christianity. That is what has to be believed.

Mere Christianity, p. 46

CHRIST, DIVINITY OF

He went about saying to people, 'I forgive your sins.' Now it is quite natural for a man to forgive something you do to *him*. Thus if somebody cheats *me* out of five pounds it is quite possible and reasonable for me to say, 'Well, I forgive him, we will say no more about it.' What on earth would you say if somebody had done *you* out of five pounds and *I* say, 'That is all right, I forgive him'? Then there is a curious thing which seems to slip out almost by accident. On one occasion this Man is sitting looking down on Jerusalem from the hill above it and suddenly in comes an extraordinary remark – 'I keep on sending you prophets and wise men.' Nobody comments on it. And yet, quite suddenly, almost incidentally, He is claiming to be the power that all through the centuries is sending wise men and leaders into the world.

God in the Dock, p. 73

We are faced, then, with a frightening alternative. This man we are talking about either was (and is) just what He said or else a lunatic, or something worse. Now it seems to be obvious that He was neither a lunatic nor a fiend: and consequently, however strange or terrifying or unlikely it may seem, I have to accept the view that He was and is God. God has landed on this enemy-occupied world in human form.

Mere Christianity, p. 44

CHRISTIAN, NEW

The senior devil, Screwtape, wrote to his nephew Wormwood with advice on how to tempt and win a human being in Wormwood's charge. 'The Enemy' is God.

It is always the novice who exaggerates. The man who has risen in society is over-refined, the young scholar is pedantic. In this new circle your patient is a novice. He is there daily meeting Christian life of a quality he never before imagined and seeing it all through an enchanted glass because he is in love. He is anxious (indeed the Enemy commands him) to imitate this quality. Can you get him to imitate this *defect* in his mistress and to exaggerate it until what was venial in her becomes in him the strongest and most beautiful of vices – Spiritual Pride?

The Screwtape Letters, p. 94

CHRISTIANITY

Christianity claims to give an account of *facts* – to tell you what the real universe is like. Its account of the universe may be true, or it may not, and once the question is really before you, then your natural inquisitiveness must make you want to know the answer. If Christianity is untrue, then no honest man will want to believe it, however helpful it might be: if it is true, every honest man will want to believe it, even if it gives him no help at all.

'Man or Rabbit?' in *God in the Dock*, pp. 59–60

I believe in Christianity as I believe that the Sun has risen, not only because I see it but because by it I see everything else.

'Is Theology Poetry?' in *Screwtape Proposes a Toast*, p. 50

I have been asked to tell you what Christians believe, and I am going to begin by telling you one thing that Christians do not need to believe. If you are a Christian you do not have to believe that all the other religions are simply wrong all through. If you are an atheist you do have to believe that the main point in all the religions of the whole world is simply one huge mistake. If you are a Christian, you are free to think that all these religions, even the queerest one, contain at least some hint of the truth. When I was an atheist I had to try to persuade myself that most of the human race have always been wrong about the question that mattered to them most; when I became a Christian I was able to take a more liberal view. But, of course, being a Christian does mean thinking that where Christianity differs from other religions, Christianity is right and they are wrong. As in arithmetic – there is only one right answer to a sum, and all other answers are wrong: but some of the wrong answers are much nearer being right than others.

Mere Christianity, p. 29

The senior devil, Screwtape, wrote to his nephew Wormwood:
Provided that meetings, pamphlets, policies, movements, causes and crusades, matter more to him than prayers and sacraments and charity, he is ours – and the more 'religious' (on those terms) the more securely ours. I could show you a pretty cageful down here.

Your affectionate uncle
SCREWTAPE

The Screwtape Letters, pp. 15–6

Christ says, 'Give me All. I don't want so much of your time and so much of your money and so much of your work: I want You. I have not come to torment your natural self, but to kill it. No half-measures are any good. I don't want to cut off a branch here and a branch there, I want to have the whole tree down. I don't want to drill the tooth, or crown it, or stop it, but to have it out. Hand over the whole natural self, all the desires which you think innocent as well as the ones you think wicked – the whole outfit. I will give you a new self instead. In fact, I will give you Myself; my own will shall become yours.'

Mere Christianity, p. 162

CHRISTLIKENESS

The more we get what we now call 'ourselves' out of the way and let Him take us over, the more truly ourselves we become ... It is no good trying to 'be myself' without Him. The more I resist Him and try to live on my own, the more I become dominated by my own heredity and upbringing and surroundings and natural desires.

Mere Christianity, pp. 185–6

CONSCIENCE

When our conscience won't come down to brass-tacks but will only vaguely accuse or vaguely approve, we must say to it, like Herbert, 'Peace, prattler' – and get on.

Letters to Malcolm: Chiefly on Prayer, p. 32

CONVERSION TO BELIEF IN GOD (1)

You must picture me alone in that room in Magdalen, night after night, feeling, whenever my mind lifted even for a second from my work, the steady, unrelenting approach of him whom I so earnestly desired not to meet. That which I greatly feared had at last come upon me. In the Trinity Term of 1929, I gave in and admitted that God was God and knelt and prayed: perhaps that night, the most dejected and reluctant convert in all England. I did not then see what is now the most shining and obvious thing, the divine humility which will accept the convert on even such terms. The prodigal son at least walked home on his own feet. But who can not duly adore that Love which will open the high gates to a prodigal who is brought in kicking, struggling, resentful, and darting his eyes in every direction for a chance to escape? These words, *compelle intrare,* compel them to come in, have been so abused by wicked men that we shudder at them; but, properly understood, they plumb the depth of the divine mercy. The hardness of God is kinder than the softness of men, and his compulsion is our liberation.

Surprised by Joy, p. 17

CONVERSION TO BELIEF IN GOD (2)

The conversion ... was only to theism, pure and simple, not to Christianity. I knew nothing yet about the Incarnation. The God to whom I surrendered was sheerly non-human ...

My conversion involved as yet no belief in a future life. I now number it among my greatest mercies that I was permitted for several months, perhaps for a year, to know God and to attempt obedience without even raising that question.

Surprised by Joy, p. 179

CONVERSION TO CHRIST

I was now approaching the source from which those arrows of Joy had been shot at me ever since childhood ... No slightest hint was vouchsafed me that there ever had been or ever would be any connection between God and Joy. If anything, it was the reverse. I had hoped that the heart of reality might be of such a kind that we can best symbolize it as a place; instead, I found it to be a Person.

Surprised by Joy, p. 179

In 1931 C.S. Lewis and his brother went the 30-mile journey from Oxford to Whipsnade Zoo on a motorbike:

I know very well when, but hardly how, the final step was taken. I was driven to Whipsnade [Zoo] one sunny morning. When we set out I did not believe that Jesus Christ is the Son of God, and when we reached the zoo I did.

Surprised by Joy, p. 184

DEATH AND RESURRECTION

In the Christian story God descends to reascend. He comes down; down from the heights of absolute being into time and space, down into humanity; down further still, if embryologists are right, to recapitulate in the womb ancient and pre-human phases of life; down to the very roots and seabed of the Nature He had created. But He goes down to come up again and bring the whole ruined world up with Him. One has the picture of a strong man stooping lower and lower to get himself underneath some great complicated burden. He must stoop in order to lift, he must almost disappear under the load before he incredibly straightens his back and marches off with the whole mass swaying on his shoulders.

Miracles, p. 117

DEVILS

There are two equal and opposite errors into which our race can fall into about the devils. One is to disbelieve in their existence. The other is to believe, and to feel an excessive and unhealthy interest in them. They themselves are equally pleased by both errors and hail a materialist or a magician with equal delight.

Preface to *The Screwtape Letters*, p. ix

DIVINITY

Divine reality is like a fugue. All His acts are different, but they all rhyme or echo to one another. It is this that makes Christianity so difficult to talk about. Fix your mind on any one story or any one doctrine and it becomes at once a magnet to which truth and glory come rushing from all levels of being. Our featureless pantheistic unities and glib rationalist distinctions are alike defeated by the seamless, yet ever-varying, texture of reality, the liveness, the elusiveness, the intertwined harmonies of the multi-dimensional fertility of God. But if this is the difficulty, it is also one of the firm grounds of our belief. To think that this was a fable, a product of our own brains as they are a product of matter would be to believe that this vast symphonic splendour had come out of something much smaller and emptier than itself. It is not so. We are nearer to the truth in the vision seen by Julian of Norwich, when Christ appeared to her holding in His hand a little thing like a hazel nut and saying, 'This is all that is created.' And it seemed to her so small and weak that she wondered how it could hold together at all.

God in the Dock, p. 17

EVANGELISM

My own work has suffered very much from the incurable intellectualism of my approach. The simple, emotional appeal ('Come to Jesus') is still often successful. But those who, like myself, lack the gift for making it, had better not attempt it.

God in the Dock, p. 94

EVIL

One of the things that surprised me when I first read the New Testament seriously was that it talked so much about a

Dark Power in the universe – a mighty evil spirit who was held to be the power behind death and disease and sin. The difference is that Christianity thinks this Dark Power was created by God, and was good when he was created, and went wrong ... it is a war between independent powers. It thinks it is a civil war, a rebellion, and we are living in part of the universe occupied by the rebel.

Enemy-occupied territory – that is what the world is. Christianity is the story of how the rightful King has landed, you might say in disguise, and is calling us all to take part in His great campaign of sabotage.

Mere Christianity, p. 37

EVOLUTIONISM

By universal evolutionism I mean the belief that the very formula of universal process is from imperfect to perfect, from small beginnings to great endings, from the rudimentary to the elaborate: the belief which makes people find it natural to think that morality springs from savage taboos, adult sentiment from infantile sexual maladjustments, thought from instinct, mind from matter, organic from inorganic, cosmos from chaos. This is perhaps the deepest habit of mind in the contemporary world. It seems to me immensely unplausible, because it makes the general course of nature so very unlike those parts of nature we can observe. You remember the old puzzle as to whether the owl came from the egg or the egg from the owl. The modern acquiescence or universal evolutionism is a kind of optical illusion, produced by attending exclusively to the owl's emergence from the egg. We are taught from childhood to notice how the perfect oak grows from the acorn and to forget that the acorn itself was dropped from a perfect oak. We are reminded constantly that the adult human being was an embryo, never that the life of the embryo came from two adult human beings. We love to notice that the express engine of today is the descendant of the 'Rocket'; we do not equally remember that the 'Rocket' springs not from some even more rudimentary engine, but from something much more perfect and complicated than itself – namely, a man of genius. The obviousness or naturalness which most people seem to find in the idea of emergent evolution thus seems to be a pure hallucination.

'Is Theology Poetry?' in *Screwtape Proposes a Toast*, p. 48

EXTREMES

The senior devil, Screwtape, wrote to his nephew Wormwood with advice on how to tempt and win a human being in Wormwood's charge. 'The Enemy' is God.

I had not forgotten my promise to consider whether we should make the patient an extreme patriot or an extreme pacifist. All extremes, except extreme devotion to the Enemy, are to be encouraged.

The Screwtape Letters, p 26

FAITH

'I have come to give myself up,' he [John] said.

'It is well,' said Mother Kirk. 'You have come a long way round to reach this place, whither I would have carried you in a few moments. But it is very well.'

'What must I do?' said John.

'You must take off your rags,' said she, 'as your friend has done already, and then you must dive into this water.'

'Alas,' he said, 'I have never learned to dive.'

'There is nothing to learn,' said she. 'The art of diving

is not to do anything new but simply to cease doing something. You have only to let yourself go.'

The Pilgrim's Regress, pp. 211–2

Now Faith ... is the art of holding on to things your reason has once accepted, in spite of your changing moods. For moods will change, whatever view your reason takes. I know that by experience. Now that I am a Christian I do have moods in which the whole thing looks very improbable ... That is why Faith is such a necessary virtue: unless you teach your moods 'where they get off', you can never be either a sound Christian or even a sound atheist, but just a creature dithering to and fro, with its beliefs really dependent on the weather and the state of its digestion. Consequently one must train the habit of Faith.

The first step is to recognize the fact that your moods change. The next is to make sure that, if you have once accepted Christianity, then some of its main doctrines shall be deliberately held before your mind for some time every day ... We have to be continually reminded of what we believe.

Mere Christianity, p. 117

I think we must introduce into the discussion a distinction between two senses of the word *Faith*. This may mean (a) a settled intellectual assent. In that sense faith (or 'belief') in

God hardly differs from faith in the uniformity of nature or in the consciousness of other people. This is what, I think, has sometimes been called a 'notional' or 'intellectual' or 'carnal' faith. It may also mean (b) a trust, or confidence, in the God whose existence is thus assented to. This involves attitude of the will. It is more like our confidence in a friend.

'Is Theism Important?' in *Compelling Reason*, pp. 149–50

FELLOWSHIP

No Christian and, indeed, no historian could accept the epigram which defines religion as 'what a man does with his solitude'. It was one of the Wesleys, I think, who said that the New Testament knows nothing of solitary religion. We are forbidden to neglect the assembling of ourselves together. Christianity is already institutional in the earliest of its documents. The Church is the Bride of Christ. We are members of one another.

'Membership' in *Fern-Seed and Elephants*, p. 1

FORGIVENESS

We say a great many things in church (and out of church too) without thinking of what we are saying. For instance, we say in the Creed 'I believe in the forgiveness of sins.' I had been saying it for several years before I asked myself why it was in the Creed. At first sight it seems hardly worth putting in. 'If one is a Christian,' I thought, 'of course one believes in the forgiveness of sins. It goes without saying.' But the people who compiled the Creed apparently thought that this was a part of our belief which we needed to be reminded of every time we went to church. And I have begun to see that, as far as I am concerned, they were right. To believe in the forgiveness of sins is not nearly so easy as I thought. Real belief in it is the sort of thing that very easily slips away if we don't keep on polishing it up.

'On Forgiveness' in *Fern-Seed and Elephants*, p. 26

Everyone says forgiveness is a lovely idea, until they have something to forgive.

Mere Christianity, p. 95

We believe that God forgives us our sins; but also that He will not do so unless we forgive other people their sins against us. There is no doubt about the second part of this statement. It is in the Lord's Prayer: it was emphatically stated by Our Lord … He doesn't say that we are to forgive other people's sins provided they are not too frightful, or provided there are extenuating circumstances, or anything of that sort. We are to forgive them all, however spiteful, however mean, however often they are repeated. If we don't, we shall be forgiven none of our own.

'On Forgiveness' in *Fern-Seed and Elephants*, pp. 26–7

FORGIVING OTHERS

Real forgiveness means looking steadily at the sin, the sin that is left over without any excuse, after all allowances have been made, and seeing it in all its horror, dirt, meanness and malice, and nevertheless being wholly reconciled to the man who has done it. That, and only that, is forgiveness; and that we can always have from God if we ask for it.

'On Forgiveness' in *Fern-Seed and Elephants*, pp. 28–9

… forgiving does not mean excusing. Many people seem to think it does. They think that if you ask them to forgive someone who has cheated or bullied them you are trying to make out that there was really no cheating or no bullying. But if that were so, there would be nothing to forgive.

'On Forgiveness' in *Fern-Seed and Elephants*, pp. 29–30

If we really want (but all depends on really wanting) to learn how to forgive, perhaps we had better start with something easier than the Gestapo. One might start with forgiving one's husband or wife; or parents or children ... for something they have done or said in the last week. That will probably keep us busy for the moment.

Mere Christianity, p. 96

To excuse what can really produce good excuses is not Christian charity; it is only fairness. To be a Christian means to forgive the inexcusable, because God has forgiven the inexcusable in you. This is hard. It is perhaps not so hard to forgive a single injury. But to forgive the incessant provocations of daily life – to keep on forgiving the bossy mother-in-law, the bullying husband, the nagging wife, the selfish daughter, the deceitful son – how can we do it? Only, I think, by remembering where we stand, by meaning our words when we say in our prayers each night, 'Forgive us our trespasses as we forgive those who trespass against us.' We are offered forgiveness on no other terms. To refuse it means to refuse God's mercy for ourselves. There is no hint of exceptions and God means what He says.

'On Forgiveness' in *Fern-Seed and Elephants*, p. 30

FREE WILL

You will notice that scripture just sails over the problem [of
the whole puzzle about grace and free will]. 'Work out your
own salvation in fear and trembling' – pure Pelagianism.
But why? 'For it is God who worketh in you' – pure
Augustinianism. It is presumably only our presuppositions
that make this appear nonsensical.

Letters to Malcolm: Chiefly on Prayer, p. 47

FRIENDSHIP

Friendship is even, if you like, angelic. But man needs to be
triply protected by humility if he is to eat the bread of angels
without risk.

The Four Loves, p. 83

FUNDAMENTALISM

I have been suspected of being what is called a Funda-
mentalist. That is because I never regard any narrative as

unhistorical simply on the ground that it includes the miraculous. Some people find the miraculous so hard to believe that they cannot imagine any reason for my acceptance of it other than a prior belief that every sentence of the Old Testament has historical or scientific truth. But this I do not hold, any more than St Jerome did when he said that Moses described Creation 'after the manner of a popular poet' (as we should say, mythically) or than Calvin did when he doubted whether the story of Job were history or fiction.

Reflections on the Psalms, p. 94

GLORY

The promise of glory is the promise, almost incredible and only possible by the work of Christ, that some of us, that any of us who really chooses, shall actually survive that examination, shall find approval, shall please God. To please God ... to be a real ingredient in the divine happiness ... to be loved by God, not merely pitied, but delighted in as an artist delights in his work or a father in a son – it seems impossible, a weight or burden of glory which our thoughts can hardly sustain. But so it is.

'The Weight of Glory' in *Screwtape Proposes a Toast*, pp. 96–7

The sense that in this universe we are treated as strangers, the longing to be acknowledged, to meet with some response, to bridge some chasm that yawns between us and reality, is part of our inconsolable secret. And surely, from this point of view, the promise of glory, in the sense described, becomes highly relevant to our deep desire. For glory meant good report with God, acceptance by God, response, acknowledgement, and welcome into the heart of things. The door on which we have been knocking all our lives will open at last.

'The Weight of Glory' in *Screwtape Proposes a Toast*, p. 98

GOD AND HUMANKIND

The relationship between God and a man is more private and intimate than any possible relation between two fellow creatures.

Letters to Malcolm: Chiefly on Prayer, p. 10

GOD, CHARACTER OF

The hardness of God is kinder than the softness of men, and his compulsion is our liberation.

Surprised by Joy, p. 178

GOD, EXISTENCE OF

There have been men before now who got so interested in proving the existence of God that they came to care nothing for God Himself ... as if the good Lord had nothing to do but *exist*! There have been some who were so occupied in spreading Christianity that they never gave a thought to Christ. Man! You see it in smaller matters. Did ye never know a lover of books that with all his first editions and signed copies had lost the power to read them? Or an organiser of charities that had lost all love for the poor? It is the subtlest of all the snares.

The Great Divorce, p. 57

GOD, NATURE OF

The Christians are not claiming that simply 'God' was incarnate in Jesus. They are claiming that the one true God is He whom the Jews worshipped as Jahweh, and that it is He who has descended. Now the double character of Jahweh is this. On the one hand He is the God of Nature, her glad Creator. It is He who sends rain into the furrows to tell the valleys to stand so thick with corn that they laugh and sing. The trees of the wood rejoice before Him and His voice causes the wild deer to bring forth their young. He is the God of wheat and wine and oil. In that respect He is constantly doing all the things that Nature-Gods do: He is Bacchus, Venus, Ceres all rolled into one. There is no trace in Judaism of the idea found in some pessimistic and Pantheistic religions that Nature is some kind of illusion or disaster, that finite existence is in itself an evil and that the cure lies in the relapse of all things into God. Compared with such anti-natural conceptions Jahweh might almost be mistaken for a Nature-God.

On the other hand, Jahweh is clearly *not* a Nature-God. He does not die and come to life each year as a true Corn-king should. He may give wine and fertility, but must not be worshipped with Bacchanalian or aphrodisiac rites. He is not the soul of Nature nor of any part of Nature. He inhabits eternity: He dwells in the high and holy place: heaven is His throne, not His vehicle, earth is His footstool, not His vesture. One day He will dismantle both and make a new heaven and earth.

Miracles, p. 120

GOD'S LOVE

We must keep always before our eyes that vision of Lady Julian's in which God carried in His hand a little object like a nut, and that nut was 'all that is made'. God, who needs nothing, loves into existence wholly superfluous creatures in order that He may love and perfect them. He creates the universe, already foreseeing – or should we say 'seeing'? There are no tenses in God – the buzzing cloud of flies about the cross, the flayed back pressed against the uneven stake, the nails driven through the mesial nerves, the repeated incipient suffocation as the body droops, the repeated torture of back and arms as it is time after time, for breath's sake, hitched up. If I may dare the biological image, God is a 'host' who deliberately creates His own parasites; causes us to be that we may exploit and 'take advantage of' Him. Herein is love. That is the diagram of Love Himself, inventor of all loves.

The Four Loves, p. 121

GOD'S POWER

His Omnipotence means power to do all that is intrinsically possible, not to do the intrinsically impossible. You may attribute miracles to him, but not nonsense. This is no limit to his power. If you choose to say 'God can give a creature free will and at the same time withhold free will from it', you have not succeeded in saying *anything* about God: meaningless combinations of words do not suddenly acquire meaning simply because we prefix to them the two other words 'God can'. It remains true that all *things* are possible with God: the intrinsic impossibilities are not things but nonentities. It is no more possible for God than for the weakest of His creatures to carry out both of two mutually exclusive alternatives; not because His power meets an obstacle, but because nonsense remains nonsense even when we talk it about God.

The Problem of Pain, p. 15

GOOD LIFE, LIVING A

The question before each of us is not 'Can *someone* lead a good life without Christianity?' The question is, 'Can *I*?' We all know there have been good men who were not Christians; men like Socrates and Confucius who had never heard of it, or men like J.S. Mill who quite honestly couldn't believe it. Supposing Christianity to be true, these men were in a state of honest ignorance or honest error. If their intentions were as good as I suppose them to have been (for of course I can't read their secret hearts) I hope and believe that the skill and mercy of God will remedy the evils which their ignorance, left to itself, would naturally produce both for them and for those whom they influenced. But the man who asks me, 'Can't I lead a good life without believing in Christianity?' is clearly not in the same position. If he hadn't heard of Christianity he would not be asking this question. If, having heard of it, and having seriously considered it, he had decided that it was untrue, then once more he would not be asking the question. The man who asks this question has heard of Christianity and is by no means certain that it may not be true. He is really asking, 'Need I bother about it? Mayn't I just evade the issue, just let sleeping dogs lie, and get on with being "good"? Aren't good intentions enough to keep me safe and blameless without knocking at that dreadful door and making sure whether there is, or isn't, someone inside?'

To such a man it might be enough to reply that he is really asking to be allowed to get on with being 'good' before he has done his best to discover what *good* means. But that is not the whole story. We need not enquire whether God will punish him for his cowardice and laziness; they will punish themselves. The man is shirking. He is deliberately trying not to know whether Christianity is true or false, because he foresees endless trouble if it should turn out to be true.

'Man or Rabbit?' in *God in the Dock*, pp. 62–3

GOOD WORK

'Good works' in the plural is an expression much more familiar to modern Christendom than 'good work'. Good works are chiefly alms-giving or 'helping' in the parish. They are quite separate from one's 'work'. And good works need not be good work, as anyone can see by inspecting some of the objects made to be sold at bazaars for charitable purposes. This is not according to our example. When our Lord provided a poor wedding party with an extra glass of wine all round, he was doing good works. But also good work; it was a wine really worth drinking. Nor is the neglect of goodness in our 'work', our job, according to precept. The apostle says everyone must not only work but work to produce what is 'good'.

'Good Work and Good Works' in
Screwtape Proposes a Toast, p. 103

GOSPELS, RELIABILITY OF

Another point is that on that view you would have to regard the accounts of the Man as being *legends*. Now, as a literary historian, I am perfectly convinced that whatever the Gospels are they are not legends. I have read a great deal of legend and I am quite clear that they are not the same sort of thing. They are not artistic enough to be legends. From an imaginative point of view they are clumsy, they don't work up to things properly. Most of the life of Jesus is totally unknown to us, as is the life of anyone else who lived at that time, and no people building up a legend would allow that to be so. Apart from bits of the Platonic dialogues, there are no conversations that I know of in ancient literature like the Fourth Gospel. There is nothing, even in modern literature, until about a hundred years ago when the realistic novel came into existence. In the story of the woman taken in adultery we are told Christ bent down and scribbled in the dust with His finger. Nothing comes of this. No one has ever based any doctrine on it. And the art of *inventing* little irrelevant details to make an imaginary scene more convincing is a purely modern art. Surely the only explanation of this passage is that the thing really happened. The author put it in simply because he had *seen* it.

God in the Dock, pp. 75–6

GRIEF

With my mother's death all settled happiness, all that was tranquil and reliable, disappeared from my life. There was to be much fun, many pleasures, many stabs of Joy; but no more of the old security. It was sea and islands now; the great continent had sunk like Atlantis.

Surprised by Joy, p. 15

HAPPINESS

In words which can still bring tears to the eyes, St Augustine describes the desolation in which the death of his friend Nebridius plunged him (*Confessions* IV, 10). Then he draws a moral. This is what comes, he says, of giving one's heart to anything but God. All human beings pass away. Do not let your happiness depend on something you may lose. If love is to be a blessing, not a misery, it must be for the only Beloved who will never pass away.

The Four Loves, p.114

HEAVEN

We find thus by experience that there is no good applying to Heaven for earthly comfort. Heaven can give heavenly comfort; no other kind. And earth cannot give earthly comfort either. There is no earthly comfort in the long run.

For the dream of finding our end, the thing we were made for, in a Heaven of purely human love could not be true unless our whole Faith were wrong. We were made for God. Only by being in some respect like Him, only by being a manifestation of His beauty, lovingkindness, wisdom or goodness, has any earthly Beloved excited our love. It is not that we have loved them too much, but that we did not quite understand what we were loving. It is not that we shall be asked to turn from them, so dearly familiar, to a Stranger. When we see the face of God we shall know that we have always known it. He has been a party to, has made, sustained and moved moment by moment within, all our earthly experiences of innocent love. All that was true love in them was, even on earth, more His than ours, and ours only because His. In Heaven there will be no anguish and no duty of turning away from our Beloved. First, because we shall have turned already; from the portraits to the Original, from the rivulets to the Fountain, from the creatures He made lovable to Love Himself. But secondly, because we shall find them all in

Him. By loving Him more than them we shall love them more than we now do.

The Four Loves, pp. 132–3

Here the whole world (stars, water, air
And field, and forest, as they were
Reflected in a single mind)
Like cast-off clothes was left behind
In ashes yet with hope that she,
Re-born from holy poverty,
In lenten lands, hereafter may
Resume them on her Easter Day.

Poems

(Epitaph for Helen Joy Davidman:
Remember HELEN JOY DAVIDMAN
D. July 1960
Loved wife of C.S. Lewis)

The faint, far-off results of those energies which God's creative rapture implanted in matter when He made the worlds are what we now call physical pleasures; and even thus filtered, they are too much for our present management. What would it be to taste at the fountain-head that stream of which even these lower reaches prove so intoxicating? Yet that, I believe, is what lies before us. As St Augustine said, the rapture of the saved soul will 'flow over' into the glorified body. In the light of our present specialized and depraved appetites, we cannot imagine this *torrens voluptatis* [torrent of pleasure], and I warn everyone most seriously not to try. But it must be mentioned, to drive out thoughts even more misleading – thoughts that what is saved is a mere ghost, or that the risen body lives in numb insensibility. The body is made for the Lord, and these dismal fancies are wide of the mark.

'The Weight of Glory' in *Screwtape Proposes a Toast*, pp. 100–1

HELL

The Dominical utterances about Hell, like all Dominical sayings, are addressed to the conscience and the will, not to our intellectual curiosity. When they have roused us into action by convincing us of a terrible possibility, they have done, probably, all they were intended to do; and if all the world were convinced Christians it would be unnecessary to say a word more on the subject.

The Problem of Pain, p. 97

I willingly believe that the damned are, in one sense, successful, rebels to the end; that the doors of hell are locked on the *inside*. I do not mean that the ghosts may not *wish* to come out of hell, in the vague fashion wherein an envious man 'wishes' to be happy: but they certainly do not will even the first preliminary stages of that self-abandonment through which alone the soul can reach any good. They enjoy forever the horrible freedom they have demanded, and are therefore self-enslaved: just as the blessed, forever submitting to obedience, become through all eternity more and more free.

The Problem of Pain, pp. 104–5

C.S. Lewis's personal secretary, Walter Hooper, laughed as he read the following inscription on a gravestone:

Here lies an atheist,
All dressed up with no place to go.

But Lewis replied, in sober mood, 'I'm sure he wishes now that were true.'

Spoken by C.S. Lewis

HERMENEUTICS (INTERPRETING LITERARY TEXTS, ESPECIALLY SCRIPTURE)

For if we once accept the doctrine of the Incarnation, we must surely be very cautious in suggesting that any circumstance in the culture of first-century Palestine was a hampering or distorting influence upon his teaching. Do we suppose that the scene of God's earthly life was selected at random? – that some other scene would have served better?

'The World's Last Night' in *Fern-Seed and Elephants*, p. 54

HOPE

Hope ... means ... a continual looking forward to the eternal world ... It does not mean that we are to leave the present world as it is. If you read history you will find that the Christians who did the most for the present world were just those who thought most of the next ... It is since Christians have largely ceased to think of the other world that they have become so ineffective in this. Aim at Heaven and you will get earth 'thrown in': aim at earth and you will get neither.

Mere Christianity, p. 111

HUMANKIND

According to that doctrine, [the doctrine of the Fall], man is now a horror to God and to himself, and a creature ill-adapted to the universe not because God made him so but because he has made himself so by the abuse of his free will. To my mind this is the sole function of the doctrine. It exists to guard against two sub-Christian theories of the origin of evil – Monism, according to which God Himself, being 'above good and evil', produced impartially the effects to which we give those two names, and Dualism, according to which God produces good, while some equal and independent power produces evil. Against both these views Christianity asserts that God is good; that He made all things good for the sake of their goodness; that one of the good things He made, namely, the free will of rational creatures, by its very nature included the possibility of evil; and that creatures, availing themselves of this possibility, have become evil.

The Problem of Pain, p. 52

'You come of the Lord Adam and the Lady Eve,' said Aslan. 'And that is both honour enough to erect the head of the poorest beggar, and shame enough to bow the shoulders of the greatest emperor in earth. Be content.'

Prince Caspian, p. 185

Human Death, according to the Christians, is a result of human sin; Man, as originally created, was immune from it: Man, when redeemed, and recalled to a new life (which will, in some undefined sense, be a bodily life) in the midst of a more organic and more fully obedient Nature, will be immune from it again. This doctrine is of course simply nonsense if a man is nothing but a Natural organism. But if he were, then, as we have seen, all thoughts would be equally nonsensical, for all would have irrational causes. Man must therefore be a composite being – a natural organism tenanted by, or in a state of *symbiosis* with, a supernatural spirit.

Miracles, p. 132

HUMILITY

Don't imagine that if you meet a really humble man he will be what most people call 'humble' nowadays: he won't be a sort of greasy, smarmy person, who's always telling you that, of course, he's nobody. Probably all you'll think about him is that he seemed a cheerful, intelligent chap who took a real interest in what you said to him. If you do dislike him, it will be because you feel a bit envious of anyone who seems to enjoy life so easily. He won't be thinking about himself at all. There I must stop.

Mere Christianity, pp. 105–6

Perfect humility dispenses with modesty.

'The Weight of Glory' in *Screwtape Proposes a Toast*, p. 96

If anyone would like to acquire humility, I can, I think, tell him the first step. The first step is to realise one is proud. And a biggish step, too. At least, nothing whatever can be done before it. If you think you are not conceited, it means you are very conceited indeed.

Mere Christianity, p. 106

IMMORTALITY

Again, Christianity asserts that every individual human being is going to live for ever, and this must be true or false. Now there are a good many things which would not be worth bothering about if I were going to live only seventy years, but which I had better bother about very seriously if I am going to live for ever. Perhaps my bad temper or my jealousy are gradually getting worse – so gradually that the increase in seventy years will not be very noticeable. But it might be absolute hell in a million years: in fact, if Christianity is true, Hell is the precisely correct technical term for what it would be. And immortality makes this other difference, which, by the by, has a connection between totalitarianism and democracy. If individuals live only seventy years, then a state, or a nation, or a civilisation, which may last for a thousand years, is more important than an individual. But if Christianity is true, then the individual is not only more important but incomparably more important, for he is everlasting and the life of a state or a civilisation, compared with his, is only a moment.

Mere Christianity, p. 61

INCARNATION

The central miracle asserted by Christians is the Incarnation. They say that God became Man. Every other miracle prepares for this, or exhibits this, or results from this. Just as every natural event is the manifestation at a particular place and moment of Nature's total character, so every particular Christian miracle manifests at a particular place and moment the character and significance of the Incarnation. There is no question in Christianity of arbitrary interferences just scattered about. It relates not a series of disconnected raids on Nature but the various steps of a strategically coherent invasion – an invasion which intends complete conquest and 'occupation'. The fitness, and therefore credibility, of the particular miracles depends on their relation to the Grand Miracle; all discussion of them in isolation from it is futile.

Miracles, p. 113

If the thing [Incarnation] happened, it was the central event in the history of the Earth – the very thing that the whole story has been about. Since it happened only once, it is by Hume's standards infinitely improbable. But then, the whole history of the Earth has also happened only once: is it therefore incredible? Hence the difficulty, which weighs upon Christian and atheist alike, of estimating the probability of the Incarnation. It is like asking whether the existence of nature herself is intrinsically probable. That is why it is easier to argue, on historical grounds, that the Incarnation actually occurred than to show, on philosophical grounds, the probability of its occurrence.

Miracles, pp. 113–4

JESUS, THE HISTORICAL

The senior devil, Screwtape, wrote to his nephew Wormwood with advice on how to tempt and win a human being in Wormwood's charge. 'The Enemy' is God.

You will find that a good many Christian-political writers think that Christianity began going wrong, and departing from the doctrine of its Founder, at a very early age. Now this idea must be used by us to encourage once again the conception of a 'historical Jesus' to be found by clearing away later 'accretions and perversions' and then to be contrasted with the whole Christian tradition. In the last generation we promoted the construction of such a 'historical Jesus' on liberal and humanitarian lines; we are now putting forward a new 'historical Jesus' on Marxian, catastrophic, and revolutionary lines. The advantages of these constructions, which we intend to change every thirty years or so, are manifold.

In the first place they all tend to direct men's devotion to something which does not exist, for each 'historical Jesus' is unhistorical. The documents say what they say and cannot be added to; each new 'historical Jesus' therefore has to be got out of them by suppression at one point and exaggeration at another, and by that sort of guessing (*brilliant* is the adjective we teach humans to apply to it) on which no one would risk ten shillings in ordinary life, but which is enough to produce a crop of new Napoleons, new Shakespeares, and new Swifts, in every publisher's autumn list.

In the second place, all such constructions place the importance of their historical Jesus in some peculiar theory He is supposed to have promulgated. He has to be a 'great man' in the modern sense of the word — one standing at the terminus of some centrifugal and unbalanced line of thought – a crank vending a panacea. We thus distract men's minds from who He is, and what He did. We first make Him solely a teacher, and then conceal the very substantial agreement between His teaching and those of all other great moral teachers. For humans must not be allowed to notice that all great moralists are sent by the Enemy not to inform men but to remind them, to restate the primeval moral platitudes against our continual concealment of them. We make the Sophists: He raises up a Socrates to answer them.

Our third aim is, by these constructions, to destroy the devotional life. For the real presence of the Enemy, otherwise experienced by men in prayer and sacrament, we substitute a merely probable, remote, shadowy, and uncouth figure, one who spoke a strange language and died a long time ago. Such an object cannot in fact be worshipped. Instead of the Creator adored by its creature, you soon have merely a leader acclaimed by a partisan, and finally a distinguished character approved by a judicious historian.

And fourthly, besides being unhistorical in the Jesus it depicts, religion of this kind is false to history in another sense. No nation, and few individuals, are really brought into the Enemy's camp by the historical study of the biography of Jesus, simply as biography. Indeed materials for a full biography have been withheld from men. The earliest converts were converted by a single historical fact (the Resurrection) and a single theological doctrine (the Redemption) operating on a sense of sin which they already had – and sin, not against some new fancy-dress law produced as a novelty by a 'great man', but against the old, platitudinous, universal moral law which they had been taught by their nurses and mothers. The 'Gospels' come later and were written not to make Christians but to edify Christians already made.

The Screwtape Letters, pp. 90-1

KNOWING GOD

If He [God] can be known it will be by self-revelation on His part, not by speculation on ours. We, therefore, look for Him where it is claimed that He has revealed Himself by miracle, by inspired teachers, by enjoined ritual. The traditions conflict, yet the longer and more sympathetically we study them the more we become aware of a common element in many of them: the theme of sacrifice, of mystical communion through the shed blood, of death and rebirth, of redemption, is too clear to escape notice.

'Religion without Dogma?' in *Compelling Reason*, p. 100

Liturgical reform

My whole liturgical position really boils down to an entreaty for permanence and uniformity. I can make do with almost any kind of service whatever, if only it will stay put. But if each form is snatched away just when I am beginning to feel at home in it, then I can never make any progress in the art of worship.

Letters to Malcolm: Chiefly on Prayer, p. 3

Love

The senior devil, Screwtape, wrote to his nephew Wormwood with advice on how to tempt and win a human being in Wormwood's charge. 'The Enemy' is God.

You complain that my last letter does not make it clear whether I regard *being in love* as a desirable state for a human or not. But really, Wormwood, that is the sort of question one expects *them* to ask! Leave them to discuss whether 'Love', or patriotism, or celibacy, or candles on altars, or teetotalism, or education, are 'good' or 'bad'. Can't you see there's no answer? Nothing matters at all except the tendency of a given state of mind, in given circumstances, to move a particular patient at a particular moment nearer to the Enemy or nearer to us. Thus it would be quite a good thing to make the patient decide that 'Love' is 'good' or 'bad'. If he is an arrogant man with a contempt for the body really based on delicacy but mistaken by him for purity – and one who takes pleasure in flouting what most of his fellows approve – by all means let him decide against love. Instil into him an overweening asceticism and then, when you have separated his sexuality from all that humanises it, weigh in on him with it in some much more brutal and cynical form. If, on the one hand, he is an emotional, gullible man, feed him on minor poets and fifth-rate novelists of the old school until you have made him believe that 'Love' is both irresistible and somehow intrinsically meritorious. This belief is not much help, I grant you, in producing casual unchastity; but it is an incomparable recipe for prolonged, 'noble', romantic, tragic adulteries, ending, if all goes well, in murders and suicides.

The Screwtape Letters, p. 75

LOVE (CHARITY)

To love at all is to be vulnerable. Love anything, and your heart will certainly be wrung and possibly be broken. If you want to make sure of keeping it intact, you must give your heart to no one, not even to an animal. Wrap it carefully round with hobbies and little luxuries; avoid all entanglements; lock it up safe in the casket or coffin of your selfishness. But in that casket – safe, dark, motionless, airless – it will change. It will not be broken; it will become unbreakable, impenetrable, irredeemable. The alternative to tragedy, or at least to the risk of tragedy, is damnation. The only place outside of Heaven where you can be perfectly safe from all the dangers and perturbations of love is Hell.

The Four Loves, p. 116

LOVE, CHRISTIAN

We need at times, some of us at most times, that Charity from others which, being Love Himself in them, loves the unlovable. But this, though a sort of love we need, is not the sort we want. We want to be loved for our cleverness, beauty, generosity, fairness, usefulness. The first hint that anyone is offering us the highest love of all is a terrible shock. This is so well recognized that spiteful people will pretend to be loving us with Charity precisely because they know that it will wound us. To say to one who expects a renewal of Affection, Friendship, or Eros, 'I forgive you as a Christian' is merely a way of continuing the quarrel. Those who say it are of course lying. But the thing would not be falsely said in order to wound unless, if it were true, it would be wounding.

The Four Loves, pp. 125–6

LOVE TOWARDS NEIGHBOURS

Do not waste time bothering whether you 'love' your neighbour; act as if you did.

Mere Christianity, p. 108

Whenever we do good to another self, just because it is a self, made (like us) by God, and desiring its own happiness as we desire ours, we shall have learned to love it a little more or, at least, to dislike it less.

Mere Christianity, pp. 108–9

MARRIAGE, CHRISTIAN

The Christian idea of marriage is based on Christ's words that a man and wife are to be regarded as a single organism – for that is what the words 'one flesh' would be in modern

English. And the Christians believe that when He said this He was not expressing a sentiment but stating a fact – just as one is stating a fact when one says that a lock and its keys are one mechanism, or that a violin and a bow are one musical instrument. The inventor of the human machine was telling us that its two halves, the male and the female, were made to be combined together in pairs, not simply on the sexual level, but totally combined.

Mere Christianity, p. 86

METAPHORS

Some people when they say that a thing is meant 'metaphorically' conclude from this that it is hardly meant at all. They rightly think that Christ spoke metaphorically when he told us to carry the cross: they wrongly conclude that carrying the cross means nothing more than leading a respectable life and subscribing moderately to charities. They reasonably think that hell 'fire' is a metaphor – and unwisely conclude that it means nothing more serious than remorse. They say that the story of the Fall in Genesis is not literal; and then go on to say (I have heard them myself) that it was really a fall upwards – which is like saying that because 'My heart is broken' contains a metaphor, it therefore means 'I feel very cheerful'. This mode of interpretation I regard, frankly, as nonsense. For me the Christian doctrines which are 'metaphorical' – or which have become metaphorical with the increase of abstract thought – mean something which is just as 'supernatural' or shocking after we have removed the ancient imagery as it was before.

Miracles, pp. 81–2

MIRACLES

The miracles in fact are a retelling in small letters of the very same story which is written across the whole world in letters too large for some of us to see. Of that larger script part is already visible, part is still unsolved. In other words, some of the miracles do locally what God has already done universally: others do locally what he has not yet done, but will do. In that sense, and from our human point of view, some are reminders and others prophecies.

God in the Dock, p. 6

When I open Ovid, or Grimm, I find the sort of miracles which really would be arbitrary. Trees talk, houses turn into trees, magic rings raise tables richly spread with food in lonely places, ships become goddesses, and men are changed into

snakes or birds or bears. It is fun to read about: the least sus-
picion that it had really happened would turn that fun into
nightmare. You find no miracles of that kind in the Gospels.
Such things, if they could be, would prove that some alien
power was invading nature; they would not in the least prove
that it was the same power which had made nature and rules
her every day. But the true miracles express not simply a god,
but God: that which is outside nature, not as a foreigner, but
as her sovereign. They announce not merely that a King has
visited our town, but that it is *the* King, *our* King.

God in the Dock, pp. 10–11

MIRACLES, THE PROBABILITY OF

One is very often asked at present whether we could not have
a Christianity stripped, or, as people who asked it say, 'freed'
from its miraculous elements, a Christianity with the miraculous elements suppressed. Now, it seems to me that precisely
the one religion in the world, or at least the only one I
know, with which you could not do that is Christianity. In a
religion like Buddhism, if you took away the miracles attrib-
uted to Gautama Buddha in some very late sources, there
would be no loss; in fact, the religion would get on very
much better without them because in that case the miracles

largely contradict the teaching. Or even in the case of a religion like Mohammedanism, nothing essential would be altered if you took away the miracles. You could have a great prophet preaching his dogmas without bringing in any miracles; they are only in the nature of a digression, or illuminated capitals. But you cannot possibly do that with Christianity, because the Christian story is precisely the story of one grand miracle, the Christian assertion being that what is beyond all space and time, what is uncreated, eternal, came into nature, into human nature, descended into His own universe, and rose again, bringing nature up with Him. It is precisely one great miracle. If you take that away there would be nothing specifically Christian left. There may be many admirable human things which Christianity shares with all other systems in the world, but there would be nothing specifically Christian. Conversely, once you have accepted that, then you will see that all other well-established Christian miracles – because, of course, there are ill-established Christian miracles; there are Christian legends just as much as there are heathen legends, or modern journalistic legends – you will see that all the well-established Christian miracles are part of it, that they all either prepare for, or exhibit, or result from the Incarnation. Just as every natural event exhibits the total character of the natural universe at a particular point and space of time; so every miracle exhibits the character of the Incarnation.

Now, if one asks whether that central grand miracle in Christianity is itself probable or improbable, of course, quite clearly you cannot be applying Hume's kind of probability. You cannot mean a probability based on statistics according to which the more often a thing has happened, the more likely it is to happen again (the more often you get indigestion from eating a certain food, the more probable it is, if you eat it again, that you again have indigestion). Certainly the Incarnation cannot be probable in that sense. It is of its very nature to have happened only once. But then it is of the very nature of the history of this world to have happened only once; and if the Incarnation happened at all, it is the central chapter of that history. It is improbable in the same way in which the whole of nature is improbable, because it is only there once, and will happen only once.

God in the Dock, pp. 48–9

MORALITY

These, then, are the two points I wanted to make. First that human beings, all over the earth, have this curious idea that they ought to behave in a certain way, and cannot really get rid of it. Secondly, that they do not in fact behave in that way. They know the Law of Nature; they break it. These two facts are the foundation of all clear thinking about ourselves and the universe we live in.

Mere Christianity, p. 7

If no set of moral ideas were truer or better than any other, there would be no sense in preferring civilised morality to savage morality, or Christian morality to Nazi morality.

The moment you say that one set of moral ideas can be better than another, you are, in fact, measuring them both by a standard, saying that one of them conforms to that standard more nearly than the other.

Mere Christianity, p. 11

Morality, then, seems to be concerned with three things. Firstly, with fair play and harmony between individuals. Secondly, with what might be called tidying up or harmonising the things inside each individual. Thirdly, with the general purpose of human life as a whole: what man was made for; what course the whole fleet ought to be on: what tune the conductor of the band wants it to play.

Mere Christianity, p. 59

MYTH

Now the story of Christ is simply a true myth: a myth working on us in the same way as the others, but with this tremendous difference that *it really happened.*

God in the Dock, p. viii

Now as myth transcends thought, Incarnation transcends myth. The heart of Christianity is a myth which is also a fact. The old myth of the Dying God, *without ceasing to be myth,* comes down from the heaven of legend and imagination to the earth of history. It *happens* – at a particular date, in a particular place, followed by definable historical consequences. We pass from a Balder or an Osiris, dying nobody knows when or where, to a historical Person crucified (it is all in order) *under Pontius Pilate.* By becoming fact it does not cease to be myth: that is the miracle. I suspect that men have sometimes derived more spiritual sustenance from myths that they did not believe than from the religion they professed. To be truly Christian we must both assent to the historical fact and also receive the myth (fact though it has become) with the same imaginative embrace which we accord to all myths. The one is hardly more necessary than the other.

God in the Dock, p. 36

NARNIA

Some people seem to think that I began by asking myself how I could say something about Christianity to children; then fixed on the fairy tale as an instrument; then collected information about child-psychology and decided what age group I'd write for; then drew up a list of basic Christian truths and hammered out 'allegories' to embody them. This is all pure moonshine. I couldn't write in that way at all. Everything began with images; a faun carrying an umbrella, a queen on a sledge, a magnificent lion. At first there wasn't even anything Christian about them; that element pushed itself in of its own accord. It was part of the bubbling.

'Sometimes Fairy Stories May Say Best What's to be Said'
in *Of Other Worlds*, p. 58

NATURE

The only imperative that nature utters is, 'Look. Listen. Attend.'

The Four Loves, p. 19

OTHER RELIGIONS

There is no half-way house and there is no parallel in other religions. If you had gone to Buddha and asked him, 'Are you the son of Bramah?' he would have said, 'My son, you are still in the vale of illusion.' If you had gone to Socrates and asked, 'Are you Zeus?' he would have laughed at you. If you had gone to Mohamed and asked, 'Are you Allah?' he would first have rent his clothes and then cut your head off. If you had asked Confucius, 'Are you Heaven?' I think he would have probably replied, 'Remarks which are not in accordance with nature are in bad taste.' The idea of a great moral teacher saying what Christ said is out of the question. In my opinion, the only person who can say that sort of thing is either God or a complete lunatic suffering from that form of delusion which undermines the whole mind of man. If you think you are a poached egg, when you are looking at a piece of toast to suit you, you may be sane, but if you think you are God, there is no chance for you. We may note in passing that He was never regarded as a mere moral teacher. He did not produce that effect on any of the people who actually met him. He produced mainly three effects – Hatred – Terror – Adoration. There was no trace of people expressing mild approval.

God in the Dock, pp. 74–5

PACIFISM

If I tried to become one [a pacifist], I should find a very doubtful factual basis, an obscure train of reasoning, a weight of authority both human and Divine against me, and strong grounds for suspecting that my wishes had directed my decision. As I have said, moral decisions do not admit of mathematical certainty. It may be, after all, that Pacifism is right. But it seems to me very long odds, longer odds that I would care to take with the voice of almost all humanity against me.

'Why I am not a Pacifist' in *Compelling Reason*, p. 16

PAIN

The human spirit will not even begin to try to surrender self-will as long as all seems to be well with it. Now error and sin both have this property, that the deeper they are the less their victim suspects their existence; they are masked evil. Pain is unmasked, unmistakable evil; every man knows that something is wrong when he is being hurt. The Masochist is no real exception. Sadism and Masochism respectively isolate, and then exaggerate, a 'moment' or 'aspect' in normal sexual passion. Sadism exaggerates the aspect of capture and domination to a point at which only ill-treatment of the beloved will satisfy the pervert -- as though he said, 'I am so much master that I even torment you.' Masochism exaggerates the complementary and opposite aspect, and says 'I am so enthralled that I welcome even pain at your hands.' Unless the pain were felt as evil – as an outrage underlining the complete mastery of the other party – it would cease, for the Masochist, to be an erotic stimulus. And pain is not only immediately recognisable evil, but evil impossible to ignore. We can rest contentedly in our sins and in our stupidities; and anyone who has watched gluttons shovelling down the most exquisite foods as if they did not know what they were eating, will admit that we can ignore even pleasure. But pain insists upon being attended to. God whispers to us in our pleasures, speaks to us in our conscience, but shouts in our pain. It is His megaphone to rouse a deaf world. A bad man, happy, is a man without the least inkling that his actions do not 'answer', that they are not in accord with the laws of the universe.

The Problem of Pain, pp. 73–4

No doubt Pain as God's megaphone is a terrible instrument; it may lead to final and unrepented rebellion. But it gives the only opportunity the bad man can have for amendment. It removes the veil; it plants the flag of truth within the fortress of a rebel soul.

If the first and lowest operation of pain shatters the illusion that all is well, the second shatters the illusion that what we have, whether good or bad in itself, is our own and enough for us. Everyone has noticed how hard it is to turn our thoughts to God when everything is going well with us. We 'have all we want' is a terrible saying when 'all' does not include God. We find God an interruption. As St Augustine says somewhere, 'God wants to give us something, but cannot, because our hands are full – there's nowhere for Him to put it.' Or as a friend of mine said, 'We regard God as an airman regards his parachute; it's there for emergencies but he hopes he'll never have to use it.' Now God, who has made us, knows what we are and that our happiness lies in Him. Yet we will not seek it in Him as long as He leaves us any other resort where it can even plausibly be looked for. While what we call 'our own life' remains agreeable we will not surrender it to Him. What then can God do in our interests but make 'our own life' less agreeable to us, and take away the plausible sources of false happiness? It is just here, where God's providence seems at first to be most cruel, that the Divine humility, the stooping down of the highest, most deserves praise. We are perplexed to see misfortune falling upon decent, inoffensive, worthy people – on capable, hard-working mothers of families or diligent, thrifty little trades-people, on those who have worked so hard, and so honestly, for their modest stock of happiness and now seem to be entering on the enjoyment of it with the fullest right.

How can I say with sufficient tenderness what here needs to be said? It does not matter that I know I must become, in the eyes of every hostile reader, as it were, personally responsible for all the sufferings I try to explain – just as, to this day, everyone talks as if St Augustine *wanted* unbaptised infants to go to Hell. But it matters enormously if I alienate anyone from the truth. Let me implore the reader to try to believe, if only for the moment, that God, who made these deserving people, may really be right when He thinks that their modest prosperity and the happiness of their children are not enough to make them blessed: that all this must fall from them in the end, and that if they have not learned to know Him they will be wretched. And therefore He troubles them, warning them in advance of an insufficiency that one day they will have to discover. The life to themselves and their families stands between them and the recognition of their need; He makes that life less sweet to them.

The Problem of Pain, pp. 76–7

All arguments in justification of suffering provoke bitter resentment against the author. You would like to know how I behave when I am experiencing pain, not writing books about it. You need not guess, for I will tell you; I am a great coward. But what is that to the purpose? When I think of pain – of anxiety that gnaws like fire and loneliness that spreads out like a desert, and the heartbreaking routine of monotonous misery, or of dull aches that blacken our whole landscape or sudden nauseating pains that knock a man's heart out at one blow, of pains that seem already intolerable and then are suddenly increased, of infuriating scorpion-stinging pains that startle into maniacal movement a man who seemed half dead with his previous tortures – it 'quite o'ercrows my spirit'. If I knew any way of escape I would crawl through the sewers to find it. But what is the good of telling you about my feelings? You know them already: they are the same as yours. I am not arguing that pain is not painful. Pain hurts. That is what the word means. I am only trying to show that the old Christian doctrine of being made 'perfect through suffering' is not incredible. To prove it palatable is beyond my design.

The Problem of Pain, pp. 84–5

'If God were good, He would wish to make His creatures perfectly happy, and if God were almighty, He would be able to do what He wished. But the creatures are not happy. Therefore God lacks either goodness, or power, or both.' This is the problem of pain, in its simplest form. The possibility of answering it depends on showing that the terms 'good' and 'almighty', and perhaps also the term 'happy', are equivocal: for it must be admitted from the outset that if the popular meanings attached to these words are the best, or the only possible, meanings, then the argument is unanswerable.

The Problem of Pain, p. 13

PATRIOTISM

Of course [healthy] patriotism ... is not in the least bit aggressive. It asks only to be let alone. It becomes militant only to protect what it loves. In any mind which has a pennyworth of imagination it produces a good attitude towards foreigners. How can I love my home without coming to realize that other men, no less rightly, love theirs?

The Four Loves, pp. 23–4

PERSONALITY

It is when I turn to Christ, when I give myself up to His Personality, that I first begin to have a real personality of my own.

Mere Christianity, p. 186

PLEASURE

If there lurks in most modern minds the notion that to desire our good and earnestly to hope for the enjoyment of it is a bad thing, I submit that this notion has crept in from Kant and the Stoics and is no part of the Christian faith. Indeed, if we consider the unblushing promises of reward and the staggering nature of the rewards promised in the Gospels, it would seem that Our Lord finds our desires not too strong, but too weak. We are half-hearted creatures, fooling about with drink and sex and ambition when infinite joy is offered us, like an ignorant child who wants to go on making mud pies in a slum because he cannot imagine what is meant by the offer of a holiday at the sea. We are far too easily pleased.

'The Weight of Glory' in *Screwtape Proposes a Toast*, pp. 87–8

PRAISE

But the most obvious fact about praise – whether of God or anything – strangely escaped me. I thought of it in terms of compliment, approval, or the giving of honour. I had never noticed that all enjoyment spontaneously overflows into praise unless (sometimes even if) shyness or the fear of boring others is deliberately brought in to check it. The world rings with praise – lovers praising their mistresses, readers their favourite poet, walkers praising the countryside, players praising their favourite game – praise of weather, wines, dishes, actors, motors, horses, colleges, countries, historical personages, children, flowers, mountains, rare stamps, rare beetles, even sometimes politicians or scholars. I had not noticed how the humblest, and at the same time most balanced and capacious, minds, praised most, while the cranks, misfits and malcontents praised least.

Reflections on the Psalms, p. 80

PRAYER

Some things are proved by the unbroken uniformity of our experiences. The law of gravitation is established by the fact that, in our experience, all bodies without exception obey it. Now even if all the things that people prayed for happened, which they do not, this would not prove what Christians mean by the efficacy of prayer. For prayer is request. The essence of request, as distinct from compulsion, is that it may or may not be granted. And if an infinitely wise Being listens to the requests of finite and foolish creatures, of course he will sometimes grant and sometimes refuse them. Invariable 'success' in prayer would not prove the Christian doctrine at all. It would prove something much more like magic – a power in certain human beings to control, or compel, the course of nature.

There are, no doubt, passages in the New Testament which may seem at first sight to promise an invariable granting of our prayers. But that cannot be what they really mean. For in the very heart of the story we meet a glaring instance to the contrary. In Gethsemane the holiest of all petitioners prayed three times that a certain cup might pass from him. It did not. After that the idea that prayer is recommended to us as a sort of infallible gimmick may be dismissed.

'The Efficacy of Prayer' in *Fern-Seed and Elephants*, pp. 79–80

And, talking of sleepiness, I entirely agree with you that no one in his senses, if he has any power of ordering his own day, would reserve his chief prayers for bedtime – obviously the worst possible hour for any action which needs concentration.

Letters to Malcolm: Chiefly on Prayer, p. 14

The ordinate frame of mind is one of the blessings we must pray for, not a fancy-dress we must put on when we pray.

Letters to Malcolm: Chiefly on Prayer, p. 21

The senior devil, Screwtape, wrote to his nephew Wormwood with advice on how to tempt and win a human being in Wormwood's charge. 'The Enemy' is God.

Whenever they are attending to the Enemy himself we are defeated, but there are ways of preventing them from doing so. The simplest is to turn their gaze away from Him towards themselves. Keep them watching their own minds and trying to produce *feelings* by the actions of their own wills. When they meant to ask Him for charity, let them, instead, start trying to manufacture charitable feelings for themselves and not notice that this is what they are doing. When they meant to pray for courage, let them really be trying to feel brave. When they say they are praying for forgiveness, let them be trying to feel forgiven. Teach them to estimate the value of each prayer by their success in producing the desired feeling; and never let them suspect how much success or failure of that kind depends on whether they are well or ill, fresh or tired, at the moment.

The Screwtape Letters, p. 14

The prayer preceding all prayer is, 'May it be the real I who speaks. May it be the real Thou that I speak to.' Infinitely various are the levels from which we pray. Emotional intensity is in itself no proof of spiritual depth. If we pray in terror we shall pray earnestly; it only proves that terror is an earnest emotion. Only God Himself can let the bucket down to the depths in us. And, on the other side, He must constantly work as the iconoclast. Every idea of Him we form, He must in mercy shatter. The most blessed result of prayer would be to rise thinking, 'But I never knew before. I never dreamed …' I suppose it was at such a moment that Thomas Aquinas said of all his own theology: 'It reminds me of straw.'

Letters to Malcolm: Chiefly on Prayer, pp. 78–9

PRAYING

The senior devil, Screwtape, wrote to his nephew Wormwood:

It is, no doubt, impossible to prevent his praying for his mother, but we have means of rendering the prayers innocuous. Make sure that they are always very 'spiritual', that he is always concerned with the state of her soul and never with her rheumatism. Two advantages will follow. In the first place, his attention will be kept on what he regards as her sins, by which, with a little guidance from you, he can be induced to mean any of her actions which are inconvenient or irritating to himself. Thus you can keep rubbing the wounds of the day a little sorer even while he is on his knees; the operation is not at all difficult and you will find it very entertaining. In the second place, since his ideas about her soul will be very crude and often erroneous, he will, in some degree, be praying for an imaginary person, and it will be your task to make that imaginary person daily less and less like the real mother – the sharp-tongued old lady at the breakfast table. In time, you may make the cleavage so wide that no thought or feeling from his prayers for the imagined mother will ever flow over into his treatment of the real one.

The Screwtape Letters, p. 10

For many years after my conversion I never used any ready-made forms [of prayer] except the Lord's Prayer. In fact I tried to pray without words at all – not to verbalise the mental acts. Even in praying for others I believe I tended to avoid their names and substituted mental images of them. I still think the prayer without words is best – if one can really achieve it. But I now see that in trying to make it my daily bread I was counting on a greater mental and spiritual strength than I really have. To pray successfully without words one needs to be 'at the top of one's form'. Otherwise the mental acts become merely imaginative or emotional acts – and a fabricated emotion is a miserable affair. When the golden moments come, when God enables one really to pray without words, who but a fool would reject the gift? But He does not give it – anyway not to me – day in, day out. My mistake was what Pascal, if I remember rightly, calls 'Error of Stoicism': thinking we can do always what we can do sometimes.

Letters to Malcolm: Chiefly on Prayer, pp. 8–9

PRIDE

If anyone thinks that Christians regard unchastity as the
supreme vice, he is quite wrong. The sins of the flesh are bad,
but they are the least bad of all sins. All the worst pleasures
are purely spiritual. The pleasure of putting other people in
the wrong, of bossing and patronizing and spoiling sport,
and backbiting; the pleasures of power, of hatred. For there
are two things inside me competing with the human self
which I must try to become. They are the Animal self, and
the Diabolical self. The Diabolical self is the worst of the
two. That is why a cold, self-righteous prig who goes regu-
larly to church may be far nearer to hell than a prostitute.
But, of course, it is better to be neither.

Mere Christianity, pp. 84–5

Pride always means enmity – it *is* enmity.

Mere Christianity, p. 102

According to Christian teachers, the essential vice, the
utmost evil, is Pride. Unchastity, anger, greed, drunkenness,
and all that, are mere fleabites in comparison: it was through
Pride that the devil became the devil: Pride leads to every
other vice: it is the complete anti-God state of mind. Does
this seem to you exaggerated? If so, think it over. I pointed

out a moment ago that the more pride one had, the more one disliked pride in others. In fact, if you want to find out how proud you are the easiest way is to ask yourself, 'How much do I dislike it when other people snub me, or refuse to take any notice of me, or shove their oar in, or patronise me, or show off?' The point is that each person's pride is in competition with everyone else's pride. It is because I wanted to be the big noise at the party that I am so annoyed at someone else being the big noise. Two trades never agree. Now what you want to get clear is that Pride is essentially competitive – is competitive by its very nature – while the other vices are competitive only, so to speak, by accident. Pride gets no pleasure out of having something, only out of having more of it than the next man. We say that people are proud of being rich, or clever, or good-looking, but they are not. They are proud of being richer, or cleverer, or better-looking than others. If everyone else became equally rich, or clever, or good-looking there would be nothing to be proud about. It is the comparison that makes you proud: the pleasure of being above the rest. Once the element of competition has gone, pride has gone. That is why I say that Pride is essentially competitive in a way the other vices are not.

Mere Christianity, pp. 100–1

PROGRESS

In my opinion, the modern conception of Progress or Evolution (as popularly imagined) is simply a myth, supported by no evidence whatever.

I say 'evolution, as popularly imagined'. I am not in the least concerned to refute Darwinism as a theorem in biology ... What I want to point out is the illegitimate transition from the Darwinian theorem in biology to the modern myth of evolutionism developmentalism or progress in general.

'The World's Last Night' in *Fern-Seed and Elephants*, p. 57

PROMISCUITY

A society in which conjugal infidelity is tolerated must always be in the long run a society adverse to women. Women, whatever a few male songs and satires may say to the contrary, are more naturally monogamous than men: it is a biological necessity. Where promiscuity prevails, they will therefore always be more often the victims than the culprits. Also, domestic happiness is more necessary to them than to us. And the quality by which they most easily hold a man, their beauty, decreases every year after they have come to maturity, but this does not happen to those qualities of personality – women don't really care twopence about our *looks* – by which we hold women. Thus in the ruthless war of promiscuity women are at a double disadvantage. They play for higher stakes and are also more likely to lose. I have no sympathy with moralists who frown at the increasing credulity of female provocativeness. These signs of desperate competition fill me with pity.

God in the Dock, p. 101

PROMISES OF SCRIPTURE

The promises of Scripture may very roughly be reduced to five heads. It is promised, firstly, that we shall be with Christ; secondly, that we shall be like Him; thirdly, with an enormous wealth of imagery, that we shall have 'glory'; fourthly, that we shall, in a sense, be fed or feasted or entertained; and, finally, that we shall have some sort of official position in the universe – ruling cities, judging angels, being pillars of God's temple.

'The Weight of Glory' in *Screwtape Proposes a Toast*, p. 93

PSALMS

Most emphatically the Psalms must be read as poems; as lyrics, with all the licences and all the formalities, the hyperboles, the emotional rather than logical connections, which are proper to lyric poetry. They must be read as poems if they are to be understood; no less than French must be read as French or English as English. Otherwise we shall miss what is in them and think we see what is not.

Reflections on the Psalms, p. 3

The most valuable thing the Psalms do for me is to express that same delight in God which made David dance. I am not saying that this is so pure or so profound a thing as the love of God reached by the greatest Christian saints and mystics. But I am not comparing it with that, I am comparing it with the merely dutiful 'churchgoing' and laborious 'saying our prayers' to which most of us are, thank God, not always, but often, reduced. Against that it stands out as something astonishingly robust, virile, and spontaneous; something we may regard with an innocent envy and may hope to be infected by as we read.

Reflections on the Psalms, pp. 39–40

REASON

The senior devil, Screwtape, wrote to his nephew Wormwood with advice on how to tempt and win a human being in Wormwood's charge. 'The Enemy' is God.

The trouble with argument is that it moves the whole struggle on to the Enemy's own ground ... By the very act of arguing, you wake the patient's reason; and once it is awake who can foresee the result? ... you will find that you have been strengthening in your patient the fatal habit of attending to universal issues and withdrawing his attention from the stream of immediate sense experiences. Your business is to fix his attention on the stream. Teach him to call it 'real life' and don't let him ask what he means by 'real'.

The Screwtape Letters, p. 2

The senior devil, Screwtape, wrote to his nephew Wormwood with advice on how to tempt and win a human being in Wormwood's charge. 'The Enemy' is God.

Remember, he is not, like you, a pure spirit. Never having been a human (Oh that abominable advantage of the Enemy's!) you don't realise how enslaved they are to the pressure of the ordinary. I once had a patient, a sound atheist, who used to read in the British Museum. One day, as he sat reading, I saw a train of thought in his mind beginning to go the wrong way. The Enemy, of course, was at his elbow in a moment. Before I knew what I was I saw my twenty years' work beginning to totter. If I had lost my head and begun to attempt a defence by argument I should have been undone. But I was not such a fool. I struck instantly at the part of the man which I had best under my control and suggested that it was just about time he had some lunch. The Enemy presumably made the counter-suggestion (you know how one can never *quite* overhear what He says to them?) that this was more important than lunch. At least I think that must have been His line for when I said 'Quite. In fact much *too* important to tackle at the end of a morning,' the patient brightened up considerably; and by the time I had added 'Much better come back after lunch and go into it with a fresh mind,' he was already halfway to the door. Once he was in the street the battle was won. I showed him a newsboy shouting the midday paper, and a No. 73 bus going past, and before he reached the bottom of the steps I had got into him an unalterable conviction that, whatever odd ideas might come into a man's head when he was shut up alone with his books, a healthy dose of 'real life' (by which he meant the bus and the newsboy) was enough to show him that all 'that sort of thing' just couldn't be true.

The Screwtape Letters, pp. 2–3

REDEMPTION

But we must not suppose that even if we succeeded in making everyone nice we should have saved their souls. A world of nice people, content in their own niceness, looking no further, turned away from God, would be just as desperately in need of salvation as a miserable world, and might be even more difficult to save.

For mere improvement is no redemption, though redemption always improves people even here and now and will, in the end, improve them to a degree we cannot yet imagine. God became man to turn creatures into sons: not simply to produce better men of the old kind but to produce a new kind of man. It is not like teaching a horse to jump better and better but like turning a horse into a winged creature. Of course, once it has got wings, it will soar over the fences which could never have been jumped and thus beat the natural horse at its own game. But there may be a period, while the wings are just beginning to grow, when it cannot do so: and at that stage the lumps on the shoulders — no one could tell by looking at them that they are going to be wings — may even give it an awkward appearance.

Mere Christianity, p. 178

REPENTANCE

Repentance … is not something God demands of you before he will take you back … It is simply a description of what going back to him is like.

Mere Christianity, p. 47

Only a bad person needs to repent: only a good person can repent perfectly. The worse you are, the more you need it and the less you can do it.

Mere Christianity, p. 47

RESURRECTION

'Oh, you're real, you're real! Oh, Aslan!' cried Lucy and both girls flung themselves upon him and covered him with kisses.

'But what does it all mean?' asked Susan when they were somewhat calmer.

'It means,' said Aslan, 'that though the Witch knew the Deep Magic, there is a magic deeper still which she did not know. Her knowledge goes back only to the dawn of Time. But if she could have looked a little further back, into the stillness and the darkness before Time dawned, she would have read there a different incantation. She would have known that when a willing victim who had committed no treachery was killed in a traitor's stead, the Table would crack and Death itself would start working backwards.'

The Lion, the Witch, and the Wardrobe, p. 148

A man really ought to say, 'The Resurrection happened two thousand years ago' in the same spirit in which he says, 'I saw a crocus yesterday.' Because we know what is coming behind the crocus. The spring comes slowly down this way; but the great thing is that the corner has been turned. There is, of course, this difference, that in the natural spring the crocus cannot choose whether it will respond or not. We can. We have the power either of withstanding the spring, and sinking back into the cosmic winter, or of going on into those 'high mid-summer pomps' in which our Leader, the Son of Man, already dwells, and to which He is calling us. It remains with us to follow or not, to die in this winter, or to go on into that spring and that summer.

God in the Dock, p. 58

The perfect surrender and humiliation were undergone by Christ: perfect because He was God, surrender and humiliation because He was man. Now the Christian belief is that if we somehow share the humility and suffering of Christ we shall also share in His conquest of death and find a new life after we have died and in it become perfect, and perfectly happy, creatures.

Mere Christianity, p. 50

REVERENCE FOR GOD

A few formal, ready-made prayers serve me as a corrective of – well, let's call it 'cheek'.

Letters to Malcolm: Chiefly on Prayer, p. 11

REWARD, ETERNAL

We must not be troubled by unbelievers when they say that this promise of reward makes the Christian life a mercenary affair. There are different kinds of reward. There is the reward which has no natural connection with the things you do to earn it, and is quite foreign to the desires that ought to accompany those things. Money is not the natural reward of love; that is why we call a man a mercenary if he married a woman for the sake of her money. But marriage is the proper reward for a real lover, and he is not mercenary for desiring it ... The proper rewards are not simply tacked on to the activity for which they are given, but are the activity itself in consummation.

'The Weight of Glory' in *Screwtape Proposes a Toast*, p. 88

SCIENCE

In science we have been reading only the notes to a poem; in Christianity we find the poem itself.

Miracles, p. 137

SECOND COMING OF CHRIST

For my own part I hate and distrust reactions not only in religion but in everything. Luther surely spoke very good sense when he compared humanity to a drunkard who, after falling off his horse on the right, falls off it the next time on the left. I am convinced that those who find in Christ's apocalyptic the whole of his message are mistaken. But a thing does not vanish – it is not even discredited – because someone has spoken of it with exaggeration. It remains exactly where it was. The only difference is that if it has recently been exaggerated, we must now take special care not to overlook it; for that is the side on which the drunk man is now most likely to fall off.

'The World's Last Night' in *Fern-Seed and Elephants*, p. 51

Perfect love, we know, casteth out fear. But so do several other things – ignorance, alcohol, passion, presumption, and stupidity. It is very desirable that we should all advance to that perfection of love in which we shall fear no longer; but it is very undesirable, until we have reached that stage, that we should allow any inferior agent to cast out our fear. The objection to any attempt at perpetual trepidation about the second coming is, in my view, quite a different one: namely, that it will certainly not succeed. Fear is an emotion: and it is quite impossible – even physically impossible – to main-tain any emotion for very long. A perpetual excitement of hope about the second coming is impossible for the same reason. Crisis-feeling of any sort is essentially transitory. Feelings come and go, and when they come a good use can be made of them: they cannot be our regular spiritual diet.

'The World's Last Night' in *Fern-Seed and Elephants*, p. 64

SEEKING CHRIST

The principle runs through all life from top to bottom. Give up yourself, and you'll find your real self. Lose your life and you'll save it. Submit to death, death of your ambitions and favourite wishes every day and death of your whole body in the end: submit with every fibre of your being, and you will find eternal life. Keep *nothing* back. Nothing that you have not given away will ever be really yours. Nothing in you that has not died will ever be raised from the dead. Look for yourself, and you will find in the long run only hatred, loneliness, despair, rage, ruin, and decay. But look for Christ and you will find Him, and with Him everything else thrown in.

Mere Christianity, p. 187

SEX, OUTSIDE MARRIAGE

The monstrosity of sexual intercourse outside marriage is that those who indulge in it are trying to isolate one kind of union (the sexual) from all other kinds of union which were intended to go along with it and make up the total union.

Mere Christianity, p. 86

SEXUAL APPETITE

You can get a large audience together for a strip-tease act — that is, to watch a girl undress on the stage. Now suppose you come to a country where you could fill a theatre by simply bringing a covered plate on to the stage and then slowly lifting the cover so as to let everyone see, just before the lights went out, that it contained a mutton chop or a bit of bacon, would you not think that in that country something had gone wrong with the appetite for food? And would not anyone who had grown up in a different world think there was something equally queer about the state of the sex instinct among us?

Mere Christianity, pp. 80–1

SEXUAL INTERCOURSE

The senior devil, Screwtape, wrote to his nephew Wormwood with advice on how to tempt and win a human being in Wormwood's charge. 'The Enemy' is God.

Now comes the joke. The Enemy described a married couple as 'one flesh'. He did not say 'a happily married couple' or 'a couple who married because they were in love', but you can make the humans ignore that. You can also make them forget that the man they call Paul did not confine it to *married* couples. Mere copulation, for him, makes 'one flesh'. You can thus get the humans to accept as rhetorical eulogies of 'being in love' what were in fact plain descriptions of the real significance of sexual intercourse. The truth is that wherever a man lies with a woman, there, whether they like it or not, a transcendental relation is set up between them which must be eternally enjoyed or eternally endured. From the true statement that this transcendental relation was intended to produce, and, if obediently entered into, too often *will* produce, affection and the family, humans can be made to infer the false belief that the blend of affection, fear, and desire which they call 'being in love' is the only thing that makes marriage either happy or holy. The error is easy to produce because 'being in love' does very often, in Western Europe, precede marriages which are made in obedience to the Enemy's designs, that is, with the intention of fidelity, fertility and good will; just as religious emotion very often, but not always, attends conversion. In other words, the humans are to be encouraged to regard as the basis for marriage a highly-coloured and distorted version of something the Enemy really promises as its result.

The Screwtape Letters, p. 71

SOVEREIGNTY OF GOD

In *Hamlet* a branch breaks and Ophelia is drowned. Did she die because the branch broke or because Shakespeare wanted her to die at that point in the play? Either – both – whichever you prefer. The alternative suggested by the question is not a real alternative at all – once you have grasped that Shakespeare is making the whole play.

God in the Dock, p. 47

SUCCESS

It is not your business to succeed, but to do right: when you have done so, the rest lies with God.

From an unpublished letter to Arthur Greeves

SUFFERING

Thomas Aquinas said of suffering, as Aristotle had said of shame, that it was a thing not good in itself; but a thing which might have a certain goodness in particular circumstances. That is to say, if evil is present, pain at recognition of the evil, being a kind of knowledge, is relatively good; for the alternative is that the soul should be ignorant of the evil, or ignorant that the evil is contrary to its nature, 'either of which', says the philosopher, 'is *manifestly* bad'. And I think, though we tremble, we agree.

The Problem of Pain, p. 100

When souls become wicked they will certainly use this possibility to turn one another; and this, perhaps, accounts for four-fifths of the sufferings of men. It is men, not God, who have produced racks, whips, prisons, slavery, guns, bayonets, and bombs; it is by human avarice or human stupidity, not by the churlishness of nature, that we have poverty and overwork.

The Problem of Pain, p. 70

TALENTS

The senior devil, Screwtape, wrote to his nephew Wormwood with advice on how to tempt and win a human being in Wormwood's charge. 'The Enemy' is God.

His [the Enemy's] whole effort, therefore, will be to get the man's mind off this subject of his own value altogether. He would rather the man thought himself a great architect or a great poet and then forget about it, than that he should spend much time and pains trying to think himself a bad one. Your efforts to instil either vainglory or false modesty into the patient will therefore be met from the Enemy's side with the obvious reminder that a man is not usually called upon to have an opinion of his own talents at all, since he can very well go on improving them to the best of his ability without deciding on his own precise niche in the temple of Fame. You must try to exclude this reminder from the patient's consciousness at all costs. The enemy will try to render real in the patient's mind a doctrine which they all profess but find difficult to bring home to their feelings – the doctrine that they did not create themselves, that their talents were given them, and that they might as well be proud of the colour of their hair. But always and by all methods the Enemy's aim will be to get the patient's mind off such questions, and your aim will be to fix it on them. Even of his sins the Enemy does not want him to think too much: once they are repented, the sooner the man turns his attention outward, the better the Enemy is pleased.

Your affection uncle
SCREWTAPE

The Screwtape Letters, pp. 55–6

TEMPTATION

He that but looketh on a plate of ham and eggs to lust after it hath already committed breakfast with it in his heart.

Letters to an American Lady

TEMPTATION, SENSUAL

I have always found that the trough periods of the human undulation provide excellent opportunity for all sensual temptations, particularly those of sex. This may surprise you, because, of course, there is more physical energy, and there-fore more potential appetite, at the peak periods; but you must remember that the powers of resistance are then also at their highest. The health and spirits which you want to use in producing lust can also, alas, be very easily used for work or play or thought or innocuous merriment. The attack has a much better chance of success when the man's whole inner world is drab and cold and empty. And it is also to be noted that the trough sexuality is subtly different in quality from that of the peak — much less likely to lead to the milk and water phenomenon which the humans call 'being in love', much more easily drawn into perversions, much less contaminated by those generous and imaginative and even spiritual concomitants which often render human sexuality so disappointing.

The Screwtape Letters, pp. 33–4

TOTAL DEPRAVITY

The doctrine of Total Depravity – when the consequence is drawn that, since we are totally depraved, our idea of good is worth simply nothing – may thus turn Christianity into a form of devil-worship.

The Problem of Pain, p. 23

TRINITY

In God's dimension, so to speak, you find a being who is three Persons while remaining one Being, just as a cube is six squares while remaining one cube.

Mere Christianity, pp. 134–5

TRUTH

One of the great difficulties is to keep before the audience's mind the question of Truth. They always think you are recommending Christianity not because it is *true* but because it is *good*. And in the discussion they will at every moment try to escape from the issue 'True – or False' into stuff about a good society, or morals, or the incomes of Bishops, or the Spanish Inquisition, or France, or Poland – or anything whatever. You have to keep forcing them back, and again back, to the real point.

'Christian Apologetics' in *Compelling Reason*, p. 75

UNIVERSE

We are inveterate poets. When a quantity is very great, we cease to regard it as mere quantity. Our imaginations awake. Instead of mere quantity, we now have a quality – the sublime. Unless this were so, the merely arithmetical greatness of the galaxy would be no more impressive than the figures in a telephone directory. It is thus, in a sense, from ourselves that the material universe derives its power to over-awe us. To a mind which did not share our emotions, and lacked our imaginative energies, the argument from size would be sheerly meaningless. Men look on the starry heavens with reverence: monkeys do not. The silence of the eternal spaces terrified Pascal, but it was the greatness of Pascal that enabled them to do so. When we are frightened by the greatness of the universe, we are (almost literally) frightened by our own shadows: for these light years and billions of centuries are mere arithmetic until the shadow of man, the poet, the maker of myth, falls upon them. I do not say we are wrong to tremble at his shadow; it is a shadow of an image of God. But if ever the vastness of matter threatens to overcross our spirits, one must remember that it is matter spiritualized which does so. To puny man, the great nebula in Andromeda owes in a sense its greatness.

God in the Dock, pp. 22–3

VIRTUE

Right actions done for the wrong reason do not help to build the internal quality or character called a 'virtue,' and it is this quality or character that really matters.

Mere Christianity, p. 84

VIVISECTION

... the most sinister thing about modern vivisection is this. If a mere sentiment justifies cruelty, why stop at a sentiment for the whole human race? There is also a sentiment for the white man against the black, for a *Herrenvolk* against the non-Aryans, for 'civilized' or 'progressive' peoples against 'savages' or 'backward' peoples. Finally, for our own country, party or class against others. Once the old Christian idea of a total difference in kind between man and beast has been abandoned, then no argument for experiments on animals can be found which is not also an argument for experiments on inferior men. If we cut up beasts simply because they cannot prevent us and because we are backing our own side in the struggle for existence, it is only logical to cut up imbeciles, criminals, enemies or capitalists for the same reasons. Indeed, experiments on men have already begun. We all hear that Nazi scientists have done them. We all suspect that our own scientists may begin to do so, in secret, at any moment.

'Vivisection' in *Compelling Reason*, p. 107

WILL, THE

Christian Love, either towards God or towards man, is an affair of the will. If we are trying to do His will we are obeying the commandments, 'Thou shalt love the Lord thy God.' He will give us feelings of love if He pleases. We cannot create them for ourselves, and we must not demand them as a right. But the great thing to remember is that, though our feelings come and go, His love for us does not. It is not wearied by our sins, or our indifference; and, therefore, it is quite relentless in its determination that we shall be cured of those sins, at whatever cost to us, at whatever cost to Him.

Mere Christianity, p. 110

WITNESSING

It may be possible for each of us to think too much of his own potential glory hereafter; it is hardly possible for him to think too often or too deeply about that of his neighbour. The load, or weight, or burden, of my neighbour's glory should be laid daily on my back, a load so heavy that only humility can carry it, and the backs of the proud will be broken. It is a serious thing to live in a society of possible gods and goddesses, to remember that the dullest and most uninteresting person you talk to may one day be a creature which, if you saw it now, you would be strongly tempted to worship – or else a horror and a corruption such as you now meet, if at all, only in a nightmare. All day long we are, in some degree, helping each other to one or other of these destinations. It is in the light of these overwhelming possibilities, it is with the awe and the circumspection proper to them, that we should conduct all our dealings with one another, all friendships, all loves, all play, all politics. There are no *ordinary* people. You have never talked to a mere mortal. Nations, cultures, arts, civilisations – these are mortal, and their life is to ours as the life of a gnat. But it is immortals whom we joke with, work with, marry, snub, and exploit – immortal horrors or everlasting splendours.

'The Weight of Glory' in *Screwtape Proposes a Toast*,
pp. 101–2

WORLDLINESS

The senior devil, Screwtape, wrote to his nephew Wormwood with advice on how to tempt and win a human being in Wormwood's charge. 'The Enemy' is God.

Prosperity knits a man to the World. He feels that he is 'finding his place in it', while really it is finding its place in him. His increasing reputation, his widening circle of acquaintances, his sense of importance, the growing pressure of absorbing and agreeable work, build up in him a sense of being really at home in earth which is just what we want. You will notice that the young are generally less unwilling to die than the middle-aged and the old.

The truth is that the Enemy, having oddly destined these mere animals to life in His own eternal world, has guarded them pretty effectively from the danger of feeling at home anywhere else. That is why we must often wish long life to our patients; seventy years is not a day too much for the difficult task of unravelling their souls from Heaven and building up a firm attachment to the earth. While they are young we find them always shooting off at a tangent. Even if we contrive to keep them ignorant of explicit religion, the incalculable winds of fantasy and music and poetry – the mere face of a girl, the song of a bird, or the sight of a horizon – are always blowing our whole structure away. They *will* not apply themselves steadily to worldly advancement, prudent connections, and the policy of safety first. So inveterate is their appetite for Heaven that our best method, at this stage, of attaching them to earth is to make them believe that earth can be turned into Heaven at some future date by politics or eugenics or 'science' or psychology, or what not.

The Screwtape Letters, p. 111

Fifty of C.S. Lewis's one-liners

The idea that prayer is recommended to us as a sort of infallible gimmick may be dismissed.

'The Efficacy of Prayer' in *Fern-Seed and Elephants*, p. 80

Next to the Blessed Sacrament itself, your neighbour is the holiest object presented to your senses.

'The Weight of Glory' in *Screwtape Proposes a Toast*, p. 102

I willingly believe that the damned are, in one sense, successful, rebels to the end; that the doors of hell are locked on the *inside*.

The Problem of Pain, pp. 104–5

The central miracle asserted by Christians is the Incarnation.

Miracles, p. 113

———o———

I believe in Christianity as I believe that the Sun has risen, not only because I see it but because by it I see everything else.

'Is Theology Poetry?' in *Screwtape Proposes a Toast*, p. 50

———o———

It is no more possible for God than for the weakest of His creatures to carry out both of two mutually exclusive alternatives.

The Problem of Pain, p. 15

———o———

Man's final conquest has proved to be the abolition of Man.

The Abolition of Man, p. 40

———o———

A society in which conjugal infidelity is tolerated must always be in the long run a society adverse to women.

God in the Dock, p. 101

My mistake was what Pascal, if I remember rightly, calls 'Error of Stoicism': thinking we can do always what we can do sometimes.

Letters to Malcolm: Chiefly on Prayer, p. 9

God whispers to us in our pleasures, speaks to us in our conscience, but shouts in our pain. It is His megaphone to rouse a deaf world.

The Problem of Pain, p. 74

Prosperity knits a man to the World.

The Screwtape Letters, p. 111

It is men, not God, who have produced racks, whips, prisons, slavery, guns, bayonets, and bombs; it is by human avarice or human stupidity, not by the churlishness of nature, that we have poverty and overwork.

The Problem of Pain, p. 70

At present, if we are reborn in Christ, the spirit in us lives directly on God.

'The Weight of Glory' in *Screwtape Proposes a Toast*, p. 100

⸺◦⸺

He is Bacchus, Venus, Ceres all rolled into one.

Miracles, p. 120

⸺◦⸺

The heart of Christianity is a myth which is also a fact.

God in the Dock, p. 36

⸺◦⸺

In science we have been reading only the notes to a poem; in Christianity we find the poem itself.

Miracles, p. 137

⸺◦⸺

The New Testament has lots to say about self-denial, but not about self-denial as an end in itself.

'The Weight of Glory' in *Screwtape Proposes a Toast*, p. 87

They [the Psalms] must be read as poems if they are to be understood.

Reflections on the Psalms, p. 3

———o———

Men look on the starry heavens with reverence: monkeys do not.

God in the Dock, p. 22

———o———

In the Christian story God descends to reascend.

Miracles, p. 117

———o———

Perfect humility dispenses with modesty.

'The Weight of Glory' in *Screwtape Proposes a Toast*, p. 96

———o———

In the Trinity Term of 1929, I gave in and admitted that God was God and knelt and prayed.

Surprised by Joy, p. 178

There are no ordinary people.

'The Weight of Glory' in *Screwtape Proposes a Toast*, p. 102

———◦———

The most valuable thing the Psalms do for me is to express that same delight in God which made David dance.

Reflections on the Psalms, p. 39

———◦———

'It means,' said Aslan, 'that though the Witch knew the Deep Magic, there is a magic deeper still which she did not know.'

The Lion, the Witch, and the Wardrobe, p. 148

———◦———

Christian Love, either towards God or towards man, is an affair of the will.

Mere Christianity, p. 110

———◦———

The Dominical utterances about Hell, like all Dominical sayings, are addressed to the conscience and the will, not to our intellectual curiosity.

The Problem of Pain, p. 97

The hardness of God is kinder than the softness of men.

Surprised by Joy, p. 178

———o———

Either this man [Jesus] was, and is, the son of God, or else a madman or something worse.

Mere Christianity, p. 43

———o———

Pride leads to every other vice: it is the complete anti-God state of mind.

Mere Christianity, p. 100

———o———

If He [God] can be known it will be by self-revelation on His part, not by speculation on ours.

'Religion without Dogma?' in *Compelling Reason*, p. 100

———o———

The obviousness or naturalness which most people seem to find in the idea of emergent evolution ... seems to be a pure hallucination.

'Is Theology Poetry?' in *Screwtape Proposes a Toast*, p. 48

There have been men before now who got so interested in proving the existence of God that they came to care nothing for God Himself.

The Great Divorce, p. 57

We are to defend Christianity itself – the faith preached by the Apostles, attested by the Martyrs, embodied in the Creeds, expounded by the Fathers.

'Christian Apologetics' in *Compelling Reason*, p. 63

There is no earthly comfort in the long run.

The Four Loves, p. 132

If we cut up beasts simply because they cannot prevent us and because we are backing our own side in the struggle for existence, it is only logical to cut up imbeciles, criminals, enemies or capitalists for the same reasons.

'Vivisection' in *Compelling Reason*, p. 107

We were made for God.

The Four Loves, p. 132

———o———

The only imperative that nature utters is, 'Look. Listen. Attend.'

The Four Loves, p. 19

———o———

But if Christianity is true, then the individual is not only more important but incomparably more important, for he is everlasting and the life of a state or a civilisation, compared with his, is only a moment.

Mere Christianity, p. 61

———o———

Conversion requires an alteration of the will, and an alteration which, in the last resort, does not occur without the intervention of the supernatural.

'The Decline of Religion' in *Compelling Reason,* p. 81

Real forgiveness means looking steadily at the sin, the sin that is left over without any excuse, after all allowances have been made, and seeing it in all its horror, dirt, meanness and malice, and nevertheless being wholly reconciled to the man who has done it.

'On Forgiveness' in *Fern-Seed and Elephants*, pp. 28–9

There have been some who were so occupied in spreading Christianity that they never gave a thought to Christ.

The Great Divorce, p. 57

It is when I turn to Christ, when I give myself up to His Personality, that I first begin to have a real personality of my own.

Mere Christianity, p. 186

So far as I can see Christianity is precisely the one religion from which the miraculous cannot be separated.

'Christian Apologetics' in *Compelling Reason*, p. 73

Christianity does not involve the belief that all things were made for man.

Miracles, p. 54

———o———

Simply to say prayers is not to pray: otherwise a team of properly trained parrots would serve as well as men.

'The Efficacy of Prayer' in *Fern-Seed and Elephants*, p. 80

———o———

I had not noticed how the humblest, and at the same time most balanced and capacious, minds, praised most, while the cranks, misfits and malcontents praised least.

Reflections on the Psalms, p. 80

———o———

A man who was merely a man and said the sort of things Jesus said would not be a great moral teacher.

Mere Christianity, p. 43

We cannot conceive how the Divine Spirit dwelled within the created and human spirit of Jesus: but neither can we conceive how His human spirit, or that of any man, dwells within his natural organism.

Miracles, p. 116

———o———

As Christ is perfect God and perfect Man, the natural loves are called to become perfect Charity and also perfect natural loves.

The Four Loves, p. 127

The last will of C.S. Lewis

IN THE NAME OF GOD, AMEN.

I, CLIVE STAPLES LEWIS Professor of the University of Cambridge hereby revoke all former wills and codicils heretofore made by me and declare this to be my last Will.

1. I APPOINT ARTHUR OWEN BARFIELD of Danes Inn House, 265 Strand in the City of Westminster, Solicitor, and ALFRED CECIL HARWOOD of South Harbour, Priory Road, Forest Row in the County of Sussex, Lecturer (hereinafter called 'my Trustees') to be the EXECUTORS AND TRUSTEES of this my Will.

2. I GIVE a legacy of £100 free of duty to each of the following persons provided that such legacies are only to be paid out of monies standing to my credit at the Bank (excluding my Royalties Account) and that if there is insufficient to pay them in full the said legacies shall abate accordingly: Maureen Helen Daisy Blake,

Laurence Harwood, Lucy Jane Barfield and Sarah Neylan.

3. I GIVE AND BEQUEATH my half share in the Portrait of Thomas Robert Hamilton which at the date hereof is hung in my rooms at Magdalene College, Cambridge to my brother Warren Hamilton Lewis for life and after his death to the Rector of St Mark's, Dundela, Strandtown, Belfast, and his successors with the request that it be hung in the F.L. Heyn Memorial Church House in the Parish of St Mark's, Dundela aforesaid.

4. I GIVE AND BEQUEATH my half share in the Portrait of Richard Lewis which at the date hereof is hung in my said rooms at Magdalene College to my said brother for life and after his death to my cousin Mrs I.W. Purvis whose address at the date hereof is c/o W.K. Bellinger, West Gardens, Boars Hill, Oxford with the request (but not so as to create any enforceable trust) that she will in due course pass on the said Portrait to such descendant of the late Richard Lewis of Ty-isa, Lower Strandtown, Belfast, as she shall deem most likely to value it.

5. SUBJECT as aforesaid I GIVE AND BEQUEATH all my books furniture and manuscripts in Magdalene College aforesaid and all my books and manuscripts in The Kilns, Headington Quarry, Oxfordshire or any house which I may be occupying at the date of my death to my said brother absolutely with the request (but not so as to create any enforceable trust) that he will allow my friends the said Arthur Owen Barfield and Alfred Cecil Harwood to take such of the said books as they wish unless he wants them for his own use and in making this request I have chiefly in mind my Greek and Latin and medieval and philosophical books.

6. I GIVE DEVISE AND BEQUEATH to my said brother absolutely all my half share in the real and leasehold property situated in Ireland which we inherited from our father.

7. (i) I DEVISE AND BEQUEATH all my real and personal estate whatsoever and wheresoever not hereby or by any codicil hereto otherwise specifically disposed of unto my Trustees Upon Trust (subject as hereinafter mentioned) to sell call in and convert the same into money with the power to postpone the sale calling in and conversion thereof so long as they shall in their absolute discretion think fit without being liable for loss and so that all income from my real and personal estate howsoever constituted or invested shall as from my death be treated as income and that a reversionary or future interest shall not be sold prior to falling into possession unless my Trustees shall see special reason for such earlier sale and that the net income of my real and personal estate for the time being remaining unsold after payment thereout or all outgoings which my Trustees shall in their absolute discretion consider payable out of income shall go and be applied as if the same were income of authorised investments or of the proceeds of an actual sale thereof.

(ii) In particular and without limiting the generality of the foregoing the copyright in any work of mine whether published or unpublished at the date of my death shall be deemed to be such an authorised investment as aforesaid so that all Royalties receivable thereon shall after payment of agent's commission and any other proper expenses be treated as income of my estate as and when the same are received.

(iii) The death duties and expenses of administering my estate shall be satisfied as far as possible out of capital assets other than copyrights Provided that if such other assets prove insufficient the balance shall be paid if reasonably possible out of current Royalties and the decision of my Trustees as to whether it is reasonably possible or not shall be final.

(iv) Subject to the provisions of the foregoing subclause no apportionment either legal or equitable shall be made between capital and income including Royalties on copyrights (which my Trustees are hereby expressly empowered to retain unsold during the life of the tenant-for-life) but any income actually received by my Trustees after my death shall belong to the tenant-for-life and any income actually received by my Trustees after the death of the tenant-for-life shall fall into and form part of the capital of my residuary estate.

8. SUBJECT as above my Trustees shall stand possessed of my residuary estate upon the following trusts, that is to say:

(1) Upon trust to pay the income to my said brother during his life.

(2) After the death of my said brother Upon Trust for each of them my stepsons David Lindsay Gresham and Douglas Howard Gresham who shall attain the age of 21 years in equal shares absolutely or if either stepson shall fail to attain the age of 21 Upon Trust as to the whole for the survivor at 21 absolutely.

9. I DECLARE that all moneys liable to be or requiring to be invested under my said Will or any Codicil thereto may be invested in any one or more of the following means of investment:

(a) In or upon any of the investments or securities in which any part of my personal estate is invested at the time of my death.

(b) Any investments from time to time sanctioned by law for the investment of trust funds.

(c) Freehold or leasehold property in Great Britain (such leasehold property having not less than sixty years unexpired at the date of such investment) whether or not the same is to be used as a residence for any beneficiary under my said Will or any Codicil thereto.

(d) Any share capital or loan capital of any Company incorporated by Royal Charter or by special Act of Parliament at Westminster or registered under the English Companies Acts and having a paid up capital of not less than £500,000 and which has in each of the three years immediately prior to the date of investment paid a dividend at the rate of at least 5 per cent per annum on its ordinary stocks and shares of which fact a letter purporting to be signed by the Secretary of the Company or by a member of the London Stock Exchange or by the Secretary or Manager or Branch Manager of a joint Stock Bank shall be sufficient evidence.

10. I DECLARE that any Executor or Trustee being a solicitor or other person engaged in any profession or business shall be entitled to be paid all professional or other charges for any business or act done by him or his firm in connection with the proof of my Will or the execution of the trusts hereof including any which an executor or trustee not being a solicitor or other persons engaged as aforesaid could have done personally.

IN WITNESS whereof I have hereunto set my hand this second day of November 1961

C.S. Lewis

SIGNED by the said CLIVE STAPLES LEWIS as his last Will in the joint presence of us who jointly at his request and in his presence have hereunto subscribed our names as witnesses:

M. Miller
15 Kiln Lane
Headington
Oxford

E. Stowell
17 Chestnut Ave
Headington
Oxford

In the High Court of Justice
The Principal Probate Registry
BE IT KNOWN that CLIVE STAPLES LEWIS of The Kilns Headington Quarry Oxford
died there on the 22nd day of November 1963
domiciled in England
AND BE IT FURTHER KNOWN that at the date hereunder written the last Will and Testament with a Codicil thereto
(a copy whereof is hereunto annexed) of the said deceased was proved and registered in the Principal Probate Registry of the

High Court of Justice and that Administration of all the estate which by law devolves to and vests in the personal representative of the said deceased was granted by the aforesaid Court to ARTHUR OWEN BARFIELD of Danes Inn House 265 Strand in the City of Westminster solicitor and ALFRED CECIL HARWOOD of South Harbour Prior Road Forest Row Sussex lecturer the executors named in the said will.

And it is hereby certified that an Inland Revenue affidavit has been delivered wherein it is shown that the gross value of the said estate in Great Britain (exclusive of what the said deceased may have been possessed of or entitled to as a trustee and not beneficially) amounts to £55,889–2–0

and that the net value of the estate amounts to £37,724–10–0.

And it is further certified that it appears by a receipt signed by an Inland Revenue officer on the said affidavit that £12,827–16–0 on account of estate duty and interest on such duty has been paid.

Dated the 1st of April 1964

Registrar

A select bibliography of C.S. Lewis's works

AUTOBIOGRAPHY

A Grief Observed (1961)
Surprised by Joy: The Shape of My Early Life (1955)

CHILDREN'S FICTION

The Horse and His Boy (1954)
The Last Battle: A Story for Children (1956)
The Lion, the Witch and the Wardrobe: A Story for Children (1950)
The Magician's Nephew (1955)
Prince Caspian: The Return to Narnia (1951)
The Voyage of the 'Dawn Treader' (1952)
The Silver Chair (1953)

ADULT FICTION

The Dark Tower and Other Stories (1977), ed. by Walter Hooper
The Great Divorce: A Drama (1945)
Out of the Silent Planet (1938)
Perelandra: A Novel (1943)
The Pilgrim's Regress: An Allegorical Apology for Christianity, Reason and Romanticism (1933)
The Screwtape Letters (1942) (with *Screwtape Proposes a Toast,* 1961)
That Hideous Strength: A Modern Fairy-Tale for Grown-Ups (1945)
Till We Have Faces: A Myth Retold (1956)

NONFICTION

The Abolition of Man; or; Reflections on Education with Special Reference to the Teaching of English in the Upper Forms of Schools (1943)
The Allegory of Love: A Study in Medieval Tradition (1936)
Beyond Personality: The Christian Idea of God (1944)
Broadcast Talks (in America, *The Case for Christianity*) (1942)
Christian Behaviour A Further Series of Broadcast Talks (1943)
The Discarded Image: An Introduction to Medieval and Renaissance Literature (1964)
English Literature in the Sixteenth Century, Excluding Drama (1954)
An Experiment in Criticism (1961)
The Four Loves (1960)

Letters to Malcolm: Chiefly on Prayer (1964)
Mere Christianity (1952)
Miracles: A Preliminary Study (1947)
The Personal Heresy: A Controversy (1939), with E.N.W. Tillyard
A Preface to 'Paradise Lost' (1942)
The Problem of Pain (1940)
Reflections on the Psalms (1958)
Spenser's Images of Life (1967), ed. by Alasdair Fowler
Studies in Words (1960)

LETTERS

Letters to an American Lady (1967), ed. by Clyde S. Kilby
Letters to Children (1985), ed. by Lyle W. Dorsett and Marjorie Lamp Mead
Letters of C.S. Lewis (1966), ed. by Warren H. Lewis
They Stand Together: The Letters of C.S. Lewis to Arthur Greeves, 1914–1963 (1979), ed. by Walter Hooper

COLLECTIONS OF ESSAYS BY C.S. LEWIS

Christian Reflections (1967), ed. by Walter Hooper
Fern-Seed and Elephants and Other Essays on Christianity (1975), ed. by Walter Hooper

God in the Dock: Essays on Theology and Ethics (1970), ed. by Walter Hooper

Of Other Worlds: Essays and Stories (1966), ed. by Walter Hooper

Present Concerns (1986), ed. by Walter Hooper

Rehabilitations and Other Essays (1939)

Selected Literary Essays (1969), ed. by Walter Hooper

Studies in Medieval and Renaissance Literature (1966), ed. by Walter Hooper

They Asked for a Paper: Papers and Addresses (1962)

Transposition and Other Addresses (in America, *The Weight of Glory*) (1949)

The Weight of Glory and Other Addresses (1980), expanded and ed. by Walter Hooper

The World's Last Night and Other Essays (1960)

POETRY

Dymer (1926) (originally published under pseudonym Clive Hamilton)

Narrative Poems (1969), ed. by Walter Hooper

Poems (1964), ed. by Walter Hooper

Spirits in Bondage: A Cycle of Lyrics (1919) (originally published under pseudonym Clive Hamilton)

BOOKS EDITED BY C.S. LEWIS

Arthurian Torso (1948)
Essays Presented to Charles Williams (1947)
George MacDonald: An Anthology (1946)

Books and letters by C.S. Lewis: a chronological list

1919

(Clive Hamilton, pseud.) *Spirits in Bondage: A Cycle of Lyrics*, London: William Heinemann, 1919. Reprint, New York, Harcourt Brace Jovanovich, 1985.

1926

(Clive Hamilton, pseud.) *Dymer*, London: J.M. Dent, 1926. Reprint, New York: Macmillan, 1950.

1933

The Pilgrim's Regress: An Allegorical Apology for Christianity, Reason, and Romanticism, London: J.M. Dent, 1933. Reprint, London: Sheed & Ward, 1944; Grand Rapids, Mich.: Eerdmans, 1958.

1936

The Allegory of Love: A Study in Medieval Tradition, Oxford: Clarendon Press, 1936.

1938

Out of the Silent Planet, London: John Lane, 1938.

1939

Rehabilitations and Other Essays, London: Oxford University Press, 1939.
The Personal Heresy: A Controversy, with E.M.W. Tillyard. London: Oxford University Press, 1939.

1940

The Problem of Pain, London: Geoffrey Bles, 1940.

1942

The Screwtape Letters, London: Geoffrey Bles, 1942. Reprinted with additional preface and new letter as *The Screwtape Letters and Screwtape Proposes a Toast*, London: Geoffrey Bles, 1961.

A Preface to 'Paradise Lost', London: Oxford University Press, 1942.

Broadcast Talks, London: Oxford University Press, 1942.

1943

Christian Behaviour: A Further Series of Broadcast Talks, London: Geoffrey Bles, 1943.

Perelandra, London: John Lane, 1943.

The Abolition of Man: Reflections on Education with Special Reference to the Teaching of English in the Upper Forms of Schools, London: Oxford University Press, 1943.

1944

Beyond Personality: The Christian Idea of God, London: Geoffrey Bles, Centenary Press, 1944.

1945

That Hideous Strength: A Modern Fairy-Tale for Grown-Ups, London: John Lane, 1945. Abridged version published as *The Tortured Planet,* New York: Avon Books, 1946.

The Great Divorce: A Dream, London: Geoffrey Bles, Centenary Press, 1945.

1947

Miracles: A Preliminary Study, London: Geoffrey Bles, 1947. Reprinted with a revised Chapter 3, London: Collins-Fontana Books, 1960.

1948

Arthurian Torso: Containing the Posthumous Fragment of the Figure of Arthur by Charles Williams and A Commentary on the Arthurian Poems of Charles Williams by C.S. Lewis, London:

Oxford University Press, 1948. Reprint, with introduction by Mary McDermott Shideler, Grand Rapids, Mich.: Eerdmans, 1974.

1949

Transposition and Other Addresses, London: Geoffrey Bles, 1949. Published in America as *The Weight of Glory and Other Addresses,* New York: Macmillan, 1949.

1950

The Lion, the Witch and the Wardrobe, London: Geoffrey Bles, 1950.

1951

Prince Caspian: The Return to Narnia, London: Geoffrey Bles, 1951.

1952

Mere Christianity, London: Geoffrey Bles, 1952. A revision and expansion of *Broadcast Talks, Christian Behaviour* and *Beyond Personality*.

The Voyage of the 'Dawn Treader', London: Geoffrey Bles, 1952.

1953

The Silver Chair, London: Geoffrey Bles, 1953.

1954

The Horse and His Boy, London: Geoffrey Bles, 1954.

English Literature in the Sixteenth Century Excluding Drama. Vol. 3 of *The Oxford History of English Literature*, Oxford: Clarendon Press, 1954.

1955

The Magician's Nephew, London: Geoffrey Bles, 1955.

Surprised by Joy: The Shape of My Early Life, London: Geoffrey Bles, 1955.

1956

The Last Battle, London: Bodley Head, 1956.
Till We Have Faces: A Myth Retold, London: Geoffrey Bles, 1956.
  New York: Harcourt, Brace & World, 1956.

1958

Reflections on the Psalms, London: Geoffrey Bles, 1958.

1960

The Four Loves, London: Geoffrey Bles, 1960.
Studies in Words, Cambridge: Cambridge University Press, 1960.
The World's Last Night and Other Essays, New York: Harcourt
  Brace & Co., 1960.

1961

(N.W. Clerk, pseud.) *A Grief Observed*, London: Faber & Faber,
  1961. Reprinted, as by C.S. Lewis, London: Faber & Faber,
  1964. Reprint (N.W. Clerk, pseud.), Greenwich, Conn.:
  Seabury Press, 1963.

An Experiment in Criticism, Cambridge: Cambridge University Press, 1961.

1962

They Asked for a Paper: Papers and Addresses, London: Geoffrey Bles, 1962

1964

Letters to Malcolm: Chiefly on Prayer, London: Geoffrey Bles, 1964.

The Discarded Image: An Introduction to Medieval and Renaissance Literature, Cambridge: Cambridge University Press, 1964.

Poems, ed. by Walter Hooper, London: Geoffrey Bles, 1964.

1965

Screwtape Proposes a Toast and Other Pieces, London: Collins-Fontana Books, 1965.

1966

Studies in Medieval and Renaissance Literature, ed. by Walter Hooper, Cambridge: Cambridge University Press, 1966.

Of Other Worlds: Essays and Stories, ed. by Walter Hooper, London: Geoffrey Bles, 1966.

Letters of C.S. Lewis, ed. by W.H. Lewis, London: Geoffrey Bless, 1966.

1967

Letters to an American Lady, ed. by Clyde Kilby, Grand Rapids, Mich.: Wm Eerdmans, 1967. Reprint, London: Hodder & Stoughton, 1969.

Christian Reflections, ed. by Walter Hooper, London: Geoffrey Bles, 1967.

1968

A Mind Awake: An Anthology of C.S. Lewis, ed. by Clyde Kilby, London: Geoffrey Bles, 1968. Reprint, New York: Harcourt, Bruce & World, 1969.

1969

Narrative Poems, ed. by Walter Hooper, London: Geoffrey Bles, 1969.

Selected Literary Essays, ed. by Walter Hooper, London: Geoffrey Bles, 1969.

1970

God in the Dock: Essays on Theology and Ethics, ed. by Walter Hooper, Grand Rapids, Mich.: Wm Eerdmans, 1970. The theological sections were published as *God in the Dock: Essays on Theology* (London: Collins-Fontana Books, 1979) and as *Undeceptions: Essays on Theology and Ethics* (London: Geoffrey Bles, 1971).

1975

Fern-Seed and Elephants and Other Essays on Christianity, ed. by Walter Hooper, London: Collins Fontana Books, 1975.

1977

The Dark Tower and Other Stories, ed. by Walter Hooper, London: Collins, 1977. New York: Harcourt Brace Jovanovich, 1977.

The Joyful Christian: Readings from C.S. Lewis, New York: Macmillan, 1977.

1979

They Stand Together: The Letters of C.S. Lewis to Arthur Greeves, 1914-63, ed. by Walter Hooper, London: Collins, 1979.

1982

On Stories, and Other Essays in Literature, ed. by Walter Hooper, London: Collins, 1982. New York: Harcourt Brace Jovanovich, 1982.

1985

Boxen: The Imaginary World of the Young C.S. Lewis, ed. by Walter Hooper, London: Collins, 1985. San Diego: Harcourt Brace Jovanovich, 1985.

Letters to Children, ed. by Lyle W. Dorsett and Marjorie Lamp Mead, New York: Macmillan, 1985.

Also available from HarperCollins *Publishers:*

C.S. Lewis: A Companion and Guide

by Walter Hooper

Clive Staples Lewis wrote some of the most enduring religious and fantasy literature of the twentieth century. His best-loved classics continue to sell in their thousands and are surpassed only by his allegorical series of children's books, based in the imaginary world of Narnia.

Now Walter Hooper, one of the world's leading scholars of C.S. Lewis's work, has written the definitive C.S. Lewis handbook. Covering every type of publication – the *Chronicles of Narnia*, science fiction, literary criticism and religion – it features among other things a chronology of the events of Lewis's life and a brief biography, detailed descriptions of the background and contents of each of Lewis's books, a 'who's who' of people in Lewis's life, a 'what's what' of locations and events and an exhaustive bibliography of all his writings.

> *It is without question the most important reference work on Lewis yet published and ... will never be entirely superseded.*
> Times Literary Supplement

> *Full of accurate scholarship, a definitive work in the most literal sense, this may well prove to be the last word on his subject.*
> Daily Telegraph

C.S. Lewis: Selected Books

This comprehensive volume contains eleven of C.S. Lewis's best-known non-fiction works, and includes:

The Four Loves
The Pilgrim's Regress
Mere Christianity
The Problem of Pain
Prayer: Letters to Malcolm
Reflections on the Psalms
The Screwtape Letters with
Screwtape Proposes a Toast
Till We Have Faces
The Great Divorce
Miracles
Surprised by Joy

Together these form a collection combining outstanding literary achievement with some of the finest Christian apologetic writing of our time, making a treasure for any serious library.

He has a quite unique power for making theology an attractive, exciting and fascinating quest.

Times Literary Supplement

C.S. Lewis: Essay Collection and other Short Pieces

Edited by Lesley Walmsley

As well as his famous theological books and the *Chronicles of Narnia*, C.S. Lewis wrote numerous essays and other short pieces in his lifetime. Most were originally published in various journals and later scattered in small collections. Now in one volume the best of the essays are brought together, celebrating once again the genius of C.S. Lewis.

In C.S. Lewis's essays we encounter this remarkable scholar in different moods: hilarious in his comic satire; passionate in his opinions; patient and dedicated as his brilliant mind works at a line of argument. The essays vary in length and complexity, depending on their subject, but all bear the marks of integrity of mind and simplicity of language. Together they demonstrate what makes Lewis's writing timeless in its appeal to all kinds of people.

C.S. Lewis: Collected Letters

Volume 1: Family Letters 1905–1931

by Walter Hooper

C.S. Lewis was a prolific letter writer and his personal correspondence reveals much of his private life, reflections, friendships and feelings. This collection, carefully chosen and arranged by Walter Hooper, is the most extensive ever published and brings together the best of C.S. Lewis's letters, some of which appear in print for the first time.

This first volume, containing family letters from 1905 to 1931, covers Lewis's boyhood and early manhood, his army years, undergraduate life at Oxford and his election to a fellowship at Magdalen College. Lewis became an atheist when he was 13 years old and his dislike of Christianity is evident in many of his letters. The volume concludes with a letter describing an evening spent with J.R.R. Tolkien and Hugo Dyson when he came to see that he was wrong to think of Christianity as one of 'many myths'. 'What Dyson and Tolkien showed me was that ... the story of Christ is simply a true myth ... but with this tremendous difference that it really happened.'